Process Improvement to Company Enrichment

Process Improvement to Company Enrichment

An Integrated Strategy

Daniel L. Plung
Connie J. Krull

BEP

BUSINESS EXPERT PRESS

Leader in applied, concise business books

Description

Process Improvement to Company Enrichment: An Integrated Strategy **presents a unique, proven methodology for achieving an environment of innovation.**

This book details a comprehensive and integrated approach to optimization: acting strategically; refining business processes; energizing personnel development; forging reasoned technology decisions; and synchronizing corporate governance, organizational design, and company culture.

Practices and principles are delivered in a conversational tone and are accompanied by intriguing historical anecdotes that entertain and help illustrate the authors' position points for each chapter—making for an interesting read.

Whether the goal is improving select aspects of your company or totally rethinking the business model, this book furnishes the roadmap for achieving that successful transformation.

Keywords

optimization; transformation; organizational design; strategic planning; process improvement; corporate restructuring; productivity enhancement; enterprise restructuring; governance; innovation

Contents

Testimonials

"Process Improvement to Company Enrichment *presents a framework for evaluating a company's strategic health and a prescription to elevate any aspect of it. As the title suggests, the narrative is all about enrichment—what it means in different business settings and how to arrive there.*

This book is not about a singular insight, general advice, or an abstract idea. Rather it delivers a concrete analytic framework and specific prescriptions for imagining, crafting, and implementing goals. The authors weave organizational science with real-life experiences and sensibilities.

Plung and Krull illuminate important truths through engaging anecdotes. They present a narrative that teaches how to think and instructions on what to do. This book is sure to educate and make the monumental task of organizational improvement appear within reach."—**K. Cunio, JD, Attorney-at-Law**

"*In sharing a vision and understanding, examining, integrating, and optimizing processes and engaging workers, the unlimited potential of an enterprise is unleashed. Enriching the company produces great value as it enriches all stakeholders. Whether a large enterprise or small business, this company enrichment process improvement book imparts wisdom to management and business leaders to be used in whole or in part.*

This book proves the statement 'Single success doesn't fulfill opportunity.' However, what it does is integrate all aspects necessary to achieve change or capture strategic opportunity using critical thinking and self-examination, while creating a culture of worker engagement."—**Terri L. Marts, CEO Marts Enterprises**

"*While artfully delving into the Operations Research foundation for its principles and precepts, this book offers a set of templates to be mixed and matched by companies in a manner that best suits the strategic business need as they move beyond* Process Improvement to Company Enrichment. *Well-crafted and impeccably supported by colorfully unforgettable historic and current situations and events, this book provides a theoretical business-based—yet entertaining and pragmatic—guide for establishing integrated, success-oriented strategic initiatives that transcend traditional continuous improvement programs and processes. Seek Enrichment here!"*—**Laurie J. Hollick, Vice President, Amentum National Security Contracts and Commercial**

Acknowledgments

We thank Vickie and Nathan for their enduring support and encouragement. We also thank Dylan for his assistance with the manuscript and Benson whose willingness to share his experience and expertise is always appreciated.

Introduction

A Perspective on Pursuing Company Enrichment

ΔΟΣ ΜΟΙ ΠΑ ΣΤΩ ΚΑΙ ΤΑΝ ΓΑΝ ΚΙΝΑΣΩ

Give me a place to stand, and I shall move the earth.

—Archimedes (287–212 BCE)

It is unlikely many of the great thinkers throughout history would contemplate making an equally grandiose pronouncement.[1] Yet, while acknowledging that "moving the earth" is hyperbole, the exaggeration can be well understood given the power Archimedes was readying to demonstrate more than 20 centuries ago. In response to a challenge from his king (Heiro II of Syracuse), Archimedes—using an arrangement of levers and pulleys he designed—proceeded, by his own hand, to launch a fully burdened ship into the sea.

However, he is much better known for two accomplishments: (1) approximating the value of pi (albeit to only four decimal places)—a feat he determined using two, 96-sided polygons, one inscribed within a circle and a second polygon that inscribed that circle and (2) having immortalized "Eureka" as the single word used to acknowledge moments of profound discovery as he had supposedly exclaimed when he solved a challenge from the king to ascertain the percentage of gold in the royal crown. As just these three diverse accomplishments attest—the use of pulleys and levers, calculating the value of pi, and formulation of the law of buoyancy—Archimedes introduced the world to a wealth of scientific and mathematical innovation.

Later challenged by that same king to build the grandest ship possible with the intent of foregoing cabotage maritime navigation in favor of traversing the Mediterranean Sea, Archimedes set to work, relying heavily on the hydrostatic principles he was to elaborate in his text,

On Floating Bodies. The outcome was the *Syracusia*, an ornately decorated and adorned ship described as 200 to 300 feet long (about one-fourth the size of a contemporary luxury liner), with the capacity to hold more than 1,500 tons of cargo and approximately 2,000 passengers and crew—a vessel so imposing that in the third century BCE (Before the Common Era), it could only be accommodated in the port of Alexandria, Egypt.[2]

Yet, when it came to translating mathematical theory and principles of physics into practical applications, Archimedes demonstrated himself to be an unparalleled military force. As poetically described in a 12th-century manuscript (*Chilades* or *Book of Histories*), for two years, instruments he designed (catapults, a giant claw-like mechanism that overturned ships, and a forerunner of the laser) held off the Roman invasion of Syracuse:

> Archimedes, at first, used machines to draw up some trading vessels,
> And having raised to the Syracusan wall the vessels
> . . ., he sent them down again to the deep all at once.
> But when Marcellus removed the vessels just a little bit,
> The old man, in turn, makes all of the Syracusans
> Able to raise stones that are large enough for each to load a wagon,
> And to sink the vessels with each man, one by one, sending down the stones.
> But as Marcellus removed those vessels by the length of a bow shot,
> The old man constructed some sort of six-angled mirror, [that]
> When the rays, later, were reflected into this,
> A fearful fiery kindling was lifted to the vessels,
> And reduced them to ashes from the length of a bow shot.[3]

Placing the range of accomplishments in perspective, it is, ultimately, Archimedes' methodology—incorporating rigorous analyses into a systematic approach to solving complex, multifaceted problems—rather than any single mathematical insight or invention—that positions him as a master in all the fields in which he endeavored. In a single sentence, one scholar aptly captures the essence of this polymath: "What emerges is a personality extraordinary for its total control of all aspects of a unified science, one which had not yet been divided up into mathematics, physics and technology."[4]

The magnitude of what Archimedes accomplished as a consequence of employing a "unified" view of science, mathematics, and technology is also the substance of the first of our three principles that underlie our strategy for promoting change.

> Principle 1: It is not the single success that marks fulfillment of opportunity in business; it is seeing and acting on all the interrelated prospects for change.

It is also this rigorous methodology that positions Archimedes as the forerunner of what was to become "operations research," the application of scientific principles and quantitative analysis as the means to derive resolutions to complex problems. In fact, in describing Archimedes' approach in holding off the Roman invasion, one text offers a description of his methodology that, in effect, is the very definition of operations research: "He collected empirical data, analyzed those data using mathematics, and used the equipment to formulate methods for countering the Roman siege."[5] And yet, a brief description of the history of operations research that he predated will illuminate how far—in one critical dimension—it has strayed from its Archimedean roots and, accordingly, why we need to employ a more practical approach in addressing the range of challenges most frequently encountered in contemporary businesses and industry.

Fortunately, or unfortunately, throughout history—as was the focus of Archimedes' final years—there has remained a constant correspondence between operations research and the art and the mechanics of conducting war. During the Renaissance and the Enlightenment, some of the greatest minds—including Leonardo Da Vinci, Michelangelo, and Galileo—applied their mathematical and scientific skills to enhancing military effectiveness. During the Napoleonic period, mathematical analyses underpinned the study of military tactics and strategies. In WW I, enhanced military machinery (tanks, submarines, and airplanes) was complemented by a range of mathematical analyses such as the "N^2" law that postulated the probability of victory in a military action based on numerical superiority, firepower superiority, and concentration of forces.

And, in a move reminiscent of King Heiro's soliciting of Archimedes to defend against the Romans, WW I saw the congressionally authorized establishment of the Naval Consulting Board, the first concerted effort formally to mobilize scientists in the aid of the military. Led by Thomas Edison, the scientists on the board, charged with solving complex naval problems, employed a methodology similar to that of Archimedes: The scientists collected empirical data from actual field operations, applied a range of scientific and mathematical techniques, and then presented their proposed solutions to the Navy. As example, the scientists "developed statistics to aid in evasion and destruction of submarines, used a 'Tactical Game Board' for solving problems of evading submarine attack, and analyzed zigzagging as a method of protecting merchant shipping against submarines."[6]

Given the breadth of analytical work that was being conducted in support of the war effort on both sides of the Atlantic, it is fitting that the term "operations research" was first used at a Royal Air Force Command Center in conjunction with a project working on refining radar-aided defense systems.[7]

As could be expected, WW II and beyond has continued to integrate scientific methodology and the scientific community into the development of more sophisticated military practices and weaponry. Perhaps the foremost example is the wealth of solicited brain power that resulted in the development of the atomic bomb. Although operations research has remained immersed in the mechanics of war, it is by this moment in time, emerging from WW II, that the concept branches out and becomes both a formal area of academic study and an established constituent of business and government.

Expanding from its military origins, operations research soon after WW II became a catchall phrase in industry and shorthand for the approach Archimedes had demonstrated in the third century BCE: methodically conducting research in pursuit of the means of making complex systems more efficient. This expansion was based largely on the work and influence of Patrick Maynard Stuart Blackett, often credited with being the "father of operations research." Having led the development of several research efforts during the war, Blackett, in his 1942 landmark essay, "Scientists at the Operational Level," was the primary agent responsible for convincing the British military leadership not only to engage scientists in the war effort but also in outlining how best to position scientists within the military structure.[8]

As a consequence, in the first two decades following WW II, the concept of operations research rapidly expanded as wartime researchers realized, just as Archimedes had demonstrated, that the basic research and implementation principles they had been refining during the war were equally applicable and readily adapted to government and industrial problems and systems (e.g., scheduling, inventory control, resource allocation, and planning). It was also the movement out from within the military complex that fostered a growth in the communication and coordination among researchers, leading—over time—to more sophisticated analytical techniques, greater computing capability, and an ever-expanding area of study and application of operations research principles.

As such, operations research quickly emerged as a course of academic study: in 1948 the Massachusetts Institute of Technology began offering a course in nonmilitary operations research techniques; four years later, the Case Institute of Technology (now Case Western Reserve University) offered master's and doctoral degrees in the discipline. That same year, the Operations Research Society of America was founded with the express purposes of (1) advancing and encouraging operations research, (2) establishing professional standards, (3) improving operational research methods and techniques, and (4) identifying useful applications of operations research. In the years since, operations research has reached into all facets of industrial relations, from business analysis to game theory and from consulting to policy analysis.

Although the contributions of operations research cannot be denied, fully appreciating the level of technical sophistication applied and the level of complexity of operational problems warranting the investment in time, resources, and capability quickly makes evident its practical limitations. To that end, let's briefly look at an operational research exercise undertaken by Delta Airlines.

As simply characterized by the operations research team chartered by the airline, Delta Airlines had a fleet assignment problem:

It has been said that an airline seat is the most perishable commodity in the world. Each time an airliner takes off with an empty seat, a revenue opportunity is lost forever. So the schedule must be designed to capture as much business as possible, maximizing revenues with as little direct operating cost as possible.

In other words, the operations research team had to figure out how to ensure the right aircraft was at the right location at the right time.[9]

The magnitude and nature of this simple sounding assignment becomes manifest when considering the myriad factors that had to be integrated into the analysis. In all, the problem represented approximately 40,000 constraints and 60,000 variables:

- Ten or more different fleets (airline types) with varying limitations: different equipment, different seating capacities, different ranges
- Approximately 30,000 flight legs (single takeoffs and landings) per day
- Approximately 30 different maintenance routines: maintenance conducted while the plane is on the tarmac awaiting its next departure and more extensive maintenance activities—for example, 757's have a 12-hour required maintenance every night
- Crew availability, including potential delays in crew arrivals and legally mandated crew breaks
- Specific airport restrictions, for example, noise restrictions, and takeoff and landing weight limitations.

At the conclusion of a multiyear effort using sophisticated linear and integer programming solvers, the system (named Coldstart by the team) was implemented, saving an estimated $200,000 per day and allowing Delta planners to determine analytically which flights need upgrades, which downgrades, cost impacts of adjustments in schedules or fleet assignments, and real-time scheduling validation and monitoring.

As the Coldstart example suggests, no longer a tool of the military, the field of operations research is now characterized as "the application of scientific methods, techniques and tools to problems involving the operations of [any] system so as to provide those in control of the system with optimum solutions to problems."[10]

And, although operations research is not the practice we recommend, this presumed adaptability of analytical techniques to unlimited industrial environments is evocative of our second principle, a direct complement and corollary to Principle 1.

Principle 2: All aspects of an enterprise are potentially subject to examination and improvement.

While operational research, as we have suggested, is a methodology with applicability to those few extremely complex challenges requiring lengthy study and sophisticated quantitative analysis, a variant of sorts that has received more widespread acceptance is Six Sigma, an approach descended from W. Edward Deming's work on statistical process control. In Six Sigma parlance, personnel are largely identified by their differing levels of training. Management, whose primary responsibilities are selecting candidates for analysis and overseeing the progress of the examination, receive limited training on Six Sigma mechanics. Successive levels of practitioners—green belts, yellow belts, and black belts—are indicative of the formal training and certifications acquired. Whereas the green and yellow belts have training in the fundamentals of quantitative analysis, black belts perform analytical analyses commensurate with that conducted by operations researchers.

However, whether engaged in operations research or Six Sigma, there is, as we have noted, a relatively insurmountable problem for most businesses. As the Delta Airlines example suggests, great gains can derive from operations research; however, the investment—in time, expertise, and cost—is in direct correspondence to the complexity of the problem under examination. Most businesses do not have problems of similar magnitude to Delta's flight assignment; nor do they have the financial resources, the in-house capability, or the time to wait on development of enhancement recommendations that may take months or years to formulate.

A case in point, at a large government contract we supported, a management push was made to introduce the use of Six Sigma. A half dozen high-performing individuals were identified to complete several months of black-belt training; a dozen or so managers were trained as Six Sigma Champions, and approximately two dozen professionals underwent yellow-belt training.

After two rounds of addressing the challenges that had instigated the management's motivation to introduce Six Sigma, the company began having difficulty identifying additional areas for black-belt analysis. Not many months after, the list of less sophisticated problems of the kind that had been worked by yellow belts also began to dry up. Despite operating an extensive array of very complicated production systems and being engaged in the development and construction of new facilities, this several hundred-million-dollar-a-year operation soon found itself without further productive use of Six Sigma. The reason, as we have been noting, was obvious.

A problem of the magnitude of the fleet assignment at Delta Airlines is not an everyday occurrence in industry—even for major corporations. The smaller the business enterprise and the less technology dependent it is, the less likely it has a sustained need or justification for the investment in or the application of operations research or Six Sigma.

All that is generally required in response to the types of challenges to advancing performance or efficiency encountered by the majority of businesses is a commitment by management to make a change; the unleashing of the workforce's expertise and experience; and a systematic and corporately endorsed method of conducting the analysis and implementing the resulting recommendations.

In this regard, it is worth remembering that prior to the introduction of operations research and Six Sigma, three of the most significant advances in industrial performance and efficiency were accomplished using the same sequence Archimedes used 20-some centuries ago: observation, a reasoned analysis, and formulation and testing of implementable actions. The achievements of Frederick Taylor, who introduced the concept of scientific management, were in large part accomplished through use of "time study men," who equipped with notebooks and stopwatches observed men doing work and then developed standards by eliminating extraneous steps in the work process. Frank and Lillian Gilbreth's introduction of ergonomics was conceived by studying images of workers' hand, eye, and foot movements recorded using stop-motion cameras. And the Hawthorne experiments that created an entire field of management theory resulted from observing how factory workers reacted to a range of changing work conditions.[11]

Even if we consider the close allegiance between the military and operations research, we cannot discount the advances directly attributable to this essential sequence of observation, systematic (noncomputational) analysis, and worker-derived resolutions. As demonstration of this fact, we only need to cite one example.

At the same time that operations research scientists were progressing toward the delivery of the atomic bomb, an equally devastating military strategy and weapon were unfolding in a remote outpost in the Utah desert.

At the Dugway Proving Grounds, a U.S. Army base, the genesis of the firebombing of Japan, the second most devastating military instrument of WW II, was formulated. At the army base, men from a nearby prison constructed a fully furnished replica of a Japanese village. Observations made during the course of bombing and rebuilding the village at least 27 times resulted in the selection of the incendiary material, the refinement of delivery requirements (e.g., height of bomb release), and the final determination to deploy the weaponry.

Immediately reminiscent of the work of Frederick Taylor (yet without the heavily, computationally oriented operations research or Six Sigma methodology), what occurred at Dugway was a demonstration of our first two principles: beginning with a sense of the complete scope of the challenge, but, at the same time, recognizing complete success is dependent on the integration and improvement of each of the component elements.

At Dugway, the constructed villages and the repetitive bombings provided the observable model; the observations translated into the means to accommodate the constraints and the variables; and the team (corporate personnel, military personnel, and scientists) reasoned what became the recommendations that culminated in the development of napalm and the firebombing of Japan.[12]

In contrast to reliance on observation and worker experience, these factors are generally considered only ancillary components of the computationally driven methodologies. Although the proponents of these approaches acknowledge that management owns the decisions and recommendations derived from the research, they minimize the role of the operators of that system in the process of determining causes and solutions. As articulated in one article summarizing the substance of operations research:

> The key here is that O.R. . . . uses a methodology that is objective and clearly articulated, and is built around the philosophy that such an approach is . . . superior to one that is based purely on subjectivity and the opinion of "experts,". . . . [it] does not preclude the use of human judgement or non-quantifiable reasoning; rather, the latter are viewed as being complementary to the analytical approach. [13]

Yet it is not hard to find major inventors throughout history who saw the exact inverse of the roles played by sophisticated analytical computation and the power of observation. As example, Charles Babbage, whose analytical engine originated the concept of digital programmable computers, offers this summation in the preface to his book, *On the Economy of Machinery and Manufactures*:

> The difficulty of understanding the processes of manufactures has unfortunately been greatly overrated. To examine them with the eye of a manufacturer, so as to be able to direct others to repeat them, does undoubtedly require much skill and previous acquaintance with the subject; but merely to apprehend their general principles and mutual relations is within the power of almost every person possessing a tolerable education.[14]

And, it should be noted, even among the originators and advocates of operations research and Six Sigma, there are calls for a more observation-based methodology. As example, C.W. Churchman, who was instrumental in establishing the graduate program in operations research at Case Institute of Technology, founded a splinter group within the Operations Research Society of America; that group promoted the concept that "every practising manager would need to master the power of the management sciences."[15] One result of this effort at balancing analysis with expertise was the launching of the journal *Management Science*, a periodical endorsing "research on the practice of management focusing on the problems, interest, and concerns of managers."[16]

Momentarily turning back to Archimedes, we need to remember the method he employed: he collected empirical data, applied a reasoned and systematic approach to its analysis, and then posited and tested its implementation. The success attested to by his approach—complemented by the engendering of the schools of scientific management, ergonomics, and management theory as just discussed—demonstrates conclusively that observation does not always need to be informed by advanced mathematical models or esoteric forms of computation.

Even looking at one of Archimedes' most technologically profound contributions, the law of buoyancy, we can see the principal underlying factor to the discovery was observation informed by reasoning—with mathematics employed to explain, not to produce, the discovery.

In "Proposition 7" in his book, *On Floating Bodies,* Archimedes explains the principle underlying the law of buoyancy as a matter of observation, illustrated in an unassuming drawing depicting the forces in effect (Figure I.1):

> A solid heavier than a fluid will, if placed in it, descend to the bottom of the fluid, and the solid will, when weighed in the fluid, be lighter than its true weight by the weight of the fluid displaced.[17]

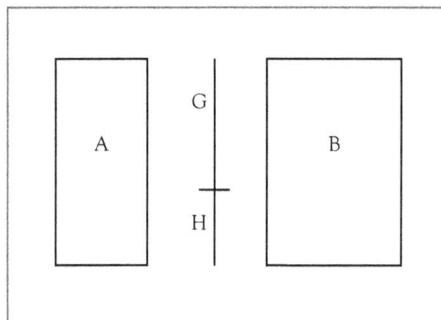

Figure I.1 Archimedes' buoyancy depiction

The bottom line is that having a unified perception of the company and recognizing that every function and program is potentially subject to analysis does not necessarily require advanced computational manipulation as a means to derive appropriate and practical avenues for process improvement. In fact, as Archimedes and advances in business and industry have demonstrated, much of what is needed can be provided by the capabilities and expertise resident in the workforce of the company or project.

Given that conclusion, there is one more principle—a principle, that when applied in concert with the other two, represents the complete scaffolding for the methodology provided in this text.

Principle 3: The methodology for enhancing operational performance should emphasize worker experience and reliance on tools and techniques that can be readily applied.

A Proven, Practical, and Ready-to-Apply Approach

According to a December 2021 publication of the U.S. Small Business Administration, there are more than 30 million small businesses in the United States—businesses with fewer than 500 employees—as opposed to just slightly more than 20,000 large businesses.[18] Our approach was developed with these "small" businesses in mind, businesses that do not have the resources for or the need to employ operations research or Six Sigma. It is a focus on businesses that can use our three principles to establish the three foundational elements to produce an integrated and comprehensive enhancement to the company:

The Vision: an orientation that encompasses the full breadth of the programs and functions that collectively comprise your company,

The Perspective: a focus on improving the individual business components while also strengthening interrelationships and interfaces, and

The Practice: a proven methodology adaptable to your company's needs, challenges, and opportunities—irrespective of its size or number of employees.

To that end, in Chapter 1 we begin with a summary of the reasoning underpinning our methodology and discuss its foundational elements. Chapter 2 examines how to conduct process reviews so as to create the springboard for enhancing other dimensions of the company infrastructure. This early focus on process improvement is one of the unique aspects of our methodology.

Whereas it might be assumed the starting point for a global reassessment should begin with discussion of the business model or business strategy, our approach begins with identifying and reworking a select number of central processes. This entry point establishes the necessary framework from which to branch outward into the other dimensions of the business: It immediately engages personnel with a range of corporate responsibilities and expertise; members of those initial teams can then bring back and introduce concepts and techniques into their respective organizations; members of the initial teams can be trained as team leaders, accelerating change throughout the organization; and it immediately establishes a common perception among management and the workforce of the process, purpose, and vision essential to sustaining a unified commitment to a global enhancement of the company.

This starting point also provides a unique impetus that derives from personnel recognizing the authority they have been given to introduce change. Laws and regulations establish boundaries and broad expectations for business and industry; they do not (and cannot) prescribe the mechanics of conducting day-to-day operations of thousands of businesses. Those practices, procedures, and policies are determined and set by the company and are—to the degree management will support—adjustable, revisable, and subject to enhancement.

It is with this understanding and in positioning personnel throughout the company prepared to support change that we then address other principal aspects of the company infrastructure: improving individual performance—through training, professional development, and reassignment; considering technological applications; re-evaluating the organizational design and company governance; and, finally, using the collective insights gathered along the way, assessing the adequacy of the company's business model, its metrics, its markets, and its strategies.

In the end, we aim to prepare you to use the power and capability your business already possesses to take advantage of the opportunity for enhancement immediately available to you—through observation and employee engagement—whether pursuing a company-wide enhancement initiative or just planning to address select aspects of the company.

We offer you a methodology that requires only two forms of investment: a management commitment to improving operational performance and a worker commitment to make full use of their expertise, experience, and initiative. Complementing those investments by applying the tools, techniques, and methodology detailed in this book will help you deliver an "Integrated Strategy" for advancing your company from "Process Improvement to Company Enrichment."

CHAPTER 1

Constructing the Agency of Change

"Public opinion," now-a-days, "is the opinion of the bald-headed man at the back of the omnibus." It is not the opinion of the aristrocratical classes . . . or of the most educated or refined classes . . . . it is simply the opinion of the ordinary mass of educated . . . mankind.

—Walter Bagehot,
The English Constitution, 1877

Recognizing that "private industry [had] begun to develop commercial launch vehicles capable of carrying human beings into space," in December 2004, Congress approved H.R. 5832, the *Commercial Space Launch Amendments Act* with the explicit goal of "safely opening space to . . . private commercial enterprises," by "[stimulating] the commercial space transportation industry." Nevertheless, manned commercial flights—as pioneered by Virgin Galactic, Blue Origin, and Space X—have only been a very recent development.

These successes—each sponsored by rich financiers—may suggest funding represented the principal impediment. However, to Congress, the primary challenge was neither financial nor technical; it was, as the *act* denotes, the need to ensure manned space flights would be conducted "safely." Reflecting a lesson imprinted on Congress's memory, the *act* anticipated that "the future of the commercial human space flight industry will depend on its ability to continually improve its safety performance."[1]

Less than a decade after President Kennedy had set the goal, the National Aeronautics and Space Administration (NASA) had safely landed the Apollo II crew on the moon. That accomplishment propelled a vision of achieving a permanent human presence in space—a vision seemingly achievable when, in 1981, NASA transitioned from single-launch vehicles to a reusable "Space Shuttle."

Yet in the process of pursuing that vision, NASA experienced two catastrophic events—the first was the deaths of three astronauts killed when an Apollo capsule, still on the ground, caught fire. The second calamity occurred two decades later on January 28, 1986.

There had been much hype surrounding the Challenger, Flight 51-L. A schoolteacher, Christa McAuliffe, had been added to the crew in large measure to symbolize the advancing democratization of space travel. The import of the accomplishment was to be announced 10 hours after liftoff in a televised conversation between Ms. McAuliffe and President Reagan during his State of the Union address. However, the Challenger was not to last 10 hours, or even 10 minutes. The Challenger blew up 73 seconds after its rockets were ignited.

Originally due to launch on January 27, the mission had been scrubbed owing to high crosswinds at the launch site. Following standard prelaunch protocols, a review was held that evening among 30 engineers and managers representing NASA and the main contractor (Thiokol) to determine whether to proceed with or delay the launch a second time. After 2½ hours of discussion and review of 13 slides addressing a range of technical issues, including the temperature at the scheduled time of launch and sealing of the O-rings that hold sections of the craft together, the engineers recommended the launch should go forward.

At 11:38 a.m. EST the following morning, the Challenger launched. The temperature was 36°F, 15° cooler than any previous launch. Within the first second of liftoff, a puff of gray smoke was visible, followed quickly by eight more puffs—indicative of grease escaping past the O-rings. Then the fuel tank, engulfed in flames, ruptured and exploded. At 73.137 seconds into its flight, traveling at a speed of Mach 1.92, and at an altitude of 46,000 feet, the Challenger was destroyed. All seven members of the crew were killed instantly.

What was learned from several of the engineers during testimony in an ensuing Congressional investigation was that the O-rings had failed to seal properly due to the launch temperature. Despite having separately considered the subjects of temperature and potential O-ring failure during their prelaunch discussion, the engineers and scientists had not considered the correspondence between those two factors. As one engineering analysis published some five years after the investigation aptly summarized: Six slides discussed by the engineers "included data on either launch temperatures or O-ring anomalies, but not both in relation to each other."[2] Moreover, NASA's prelaunch checklists, the final determinant of whether to launch, made no reference to launch temperature.

The loss of the Challenger, in the simplest terms, was a failure—by ostensibly the most knowledgeable team possible—to look across the full spectrum of possibilities. It was also, to a lesser degree, a question of whether NASA had assembled an evaluation team with a broad enough mindset.

This narrowing of focus and perspective points to the significance of fully appreciating the predicates that underlie all three principles we established in the Introduction: ensuring the completeness of the field of vision and the integrity of decision-making process applied by the team entrusted with identifying and enhancing the interrelated opportunities for company enrichment.

A Company in Perspective

There are many ways to categorize a company. At a basic level, companies are a compilation of a network of four broad categories of functions: (1) core work functions that provide for the operation and maintenance of the equipment, systems, and facilities that produce the company's products; (2) enabling functions that provide essential infrastructure to the operations and projects areas, such as training, project controls, safety, and quality assurance; (3) improvement functions, such as internal audit and business assurance, that ensure accountability is maintained and processes are not only compliant with requirements and regulations but also performing efficiently; and (4) management functions that provide for the day-to-day business and administrative support, such as finance, human resources, and procurement (Figure 1.1).

Cutting across these organizational structures are the overarching business drivers that collectively focus on the company's health and sustainability: lowering costs, reducing risks, improving customer satisfaction, simplifying operations, and improving quality and process consistency.

Generic Corporate Focus

| Core Work Functions | Enabling Functions | Improvement Functions | Management Functions |

Generic Corporate Structure

Projects and Operations

Managing, operating, and maintaining equipment, facilities, projects, and production systems

Operational Support

Functions in direct support of projects and operations: project controls, training, safety

Managing the Business

Programs that ensure accountability and transparency, e.g., internal audit, quality assurance

Business and Administrative Services

General support and overhead functions, e.g., human resources

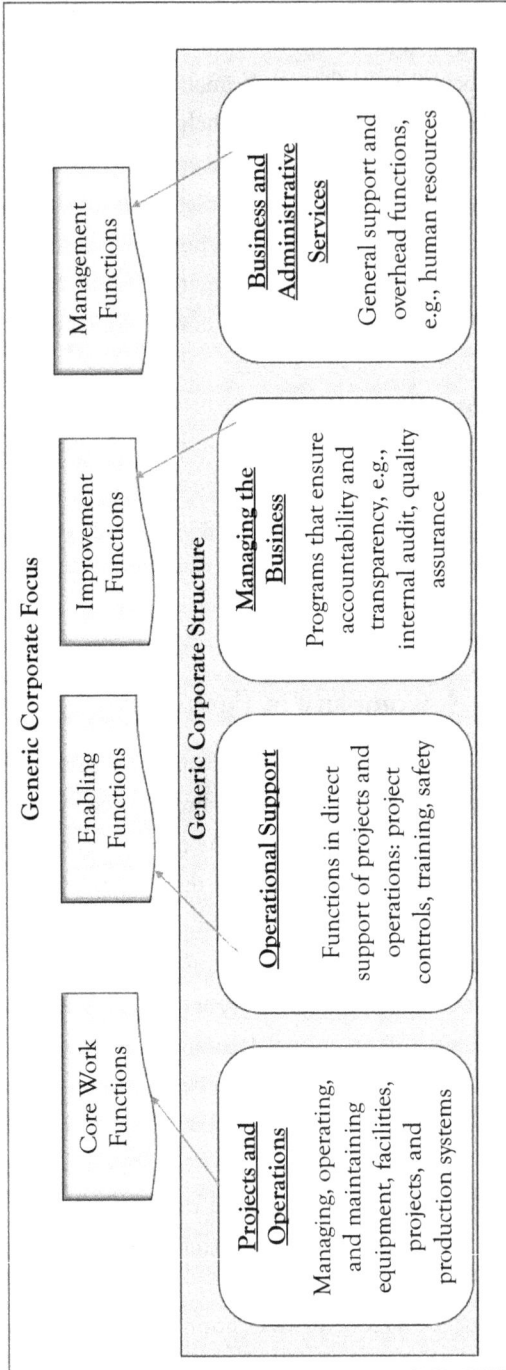

Figure 1.1 Representation of a basic corporate structure

Irrespective of how the company is structured, and independent of its size and complexity, experience has shown us that there are five common attributes that must remain a central focus of the company if it is to provide the fundamentals of sustainability as well as remain responsive to customer demands, competition, and the continual challenges of the marketplace. These five factors are also the predicates of corporate enrichment, and, as such, together represent the foundations of change:

1. Envisioning the possibilities
2. Marshaling the resources
3. Securing an effective team culture
4. Taking a disciplined approach to selecting team members
5. Instituting a formal approach to decision making

Envisioning the Possibilities

Beginning with a single process, the company has opportunity to pursue changes that span out throughout the body of the organization. The basis for expanding from a single point of improvement outwards to the realization of a more distributed and more encompassing breadth of improvement entails a series of potential enrichment categories:

- Examining opportunities in improving the performance of processes
- Identifying the means to strengthen the workforce
- Re-evaluating whether there are more efficient, more productive means to conduct and automate facets of the business
- Reconsidering how to minimize the number and complexity of interfaces
- Determining whether the controls imposed on the various operations and functions are providing an appropriate level of governance or are hindering the performance and initiative of the company and its workforce (Figure 1.2)

Accomplishing these objectives requires re-evaluating conventions and how work is done, reconsidering the levels and methods of oversight, and aligning the capabilities of the individual workers with their assignments (Table 1.1). Although the sequence in which these areas are addressed is somewhat mutable, we have found that a single process that is widely thought by the employees to be in need of improvement is the best starting point. Not only are people likely to accept change, but the work processes represent the basic framework of the company and have embedded within them decisions reflecting the other enrichment factors: reliance on technology, investment in personnel training and development, the nature of applied governance, and even suggestions about the company strategy (e.g., how the company has chosen to respond to regulations).

Even before developing a plan to review individual processes, it is helpful to conduct a basic assessment of the company's initial positioning as regards the status of these enrichment factors. For simplicity's sake, we might consider four levels of enrichment. At the level offering the greatest opportunity for enrichment is the company that has segregated the various functions; relies extensively on manual processes; is not given to careful, disciplined assessment or self-evaluation; and, in instances where expertise or effective controls do exist, they are only applied locally and

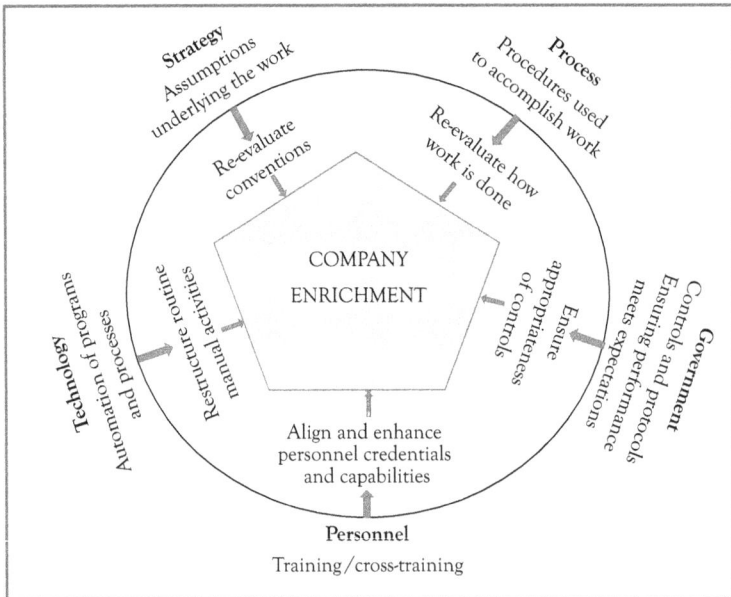

Figure 1.2 A comprehensive approach to enrichment

Table 1.1 Enrichment overview

Enrichment Focal Area	Potential Opportunities
Process	Focus on procedures identified as warranting improvements as reported in assessments, reviews, and reports
Strategy	Review assumptions employed in decision making
Technology	Identify highly labor-intensive and repetitive tasks
Personnel performance	Assess personnel productivity—cross-training, temporary assignments, mentoring
Controls and governance	Re-examine review and approval processes, business metrics, and business controls

do not benefit the company as a whole. At the other end of the spectrum, as one might expect, is the company that has rigorously attended to optimizing operations; applies expertise and systems that reach across program boundaries; grows talent and needed expertise internally; and monitors and delineates the mechanics needed for continuous improvement, oversight, and decision making (Table 1.2).

The goal for any company committed to improving corporate performance is to continue to advance through the stages from one level to the next, always aspiring to attain the "enhanced" level for each of the focus areas. However, advances in enhancement do not occur necessarily across all the focal points at the same time or at the same pace. More than likely, even a company that has several "segregated" components will also have components in the "integrated" or "process-driven" columns. This is generally due to the fact that even a company that does not commit to or even actively endorse improvement will have a complement of personnel who on their own initiative will improve processes, bring in fresh ideas, or do a better job of mentoring and training their personnel. It is also unlikely because companies at that lowest level of enrichment scale are most likely not prepared to meet the long-term challenges needed to keep the company afloat.

Yet, at the same time, it is also not likely that a company will achieve an "enhanced" status in all categories. This corollary to the situation of a company that has achieved limited enhancement is a consequence of naturally occurring market conditions. New technology is always on the horizon; markets routinely rise and fall; customer expectations change;

Table 1.2 Company enrichment scale

Focal Points	Segregated Components	Integrated	Process Driven	Enhanced
Strategy	• Programs individually focused on cost and efficiency • Limited capability to respond to market changes	• Limited cross-functional coordination	• Business processes are foundational elements of the company	• Optimized systems and processes • Adaptive to market changes and dynamics
Process	• Static operations, with limited routine re-evaluation	• Limited efforts at cross-system enhancements or redefinition	• Incorporates formal mechanisms for quality control and performance monitoring	• Processes integrated across company; improvement approaches, e.g., statistical process control routinely applied
Technology	• Minimal utilization of technical applications	• Infrastructure systems (e.g., procurement) are automated, and basic performance monitoring capability in place	• Routine improvement programs used to identify applications and process that can be automated and streamlined	• Cross-functional applications/enterprise systems implemented, along with software quality control tools
Personnel	• Individual pockets of subject matter experts • Limited resource sharing or personnel development	• Limited understanding or attention to cross-functional opportunities to assign, mentor, and develop personnel	• Cross-functional teams deployed to address opportunities for performance/product enhancement	• Training, developing, and mentoring programs in place and highly utilized • Focus on internal promotions and advancement of personnel
Governance	• Procedures and policies set independently on a program-by-program, process-by-process basis	• Cross-department initiatives are in place to address program interfaces	• Focus on data management and integrity, as well as formulation of company-wide policies for safety, technical, and business processes	• Policies established for business practices and for high-level (including corporate) decision making

and the nature and magnitudes of specific risks associated with various segments of the economy are persistently susceptible to multiple fluctuating forces.

In other words, as a company seeks to enhance itself, it is continually challenged by factors—especially in the areas of technology, processes, and personnel—challenges that would, unless aggressively countered, degrade the company's status (i.e., draw it to the left on the enhancement scale). As reported in a 2021 "Risk Barometer" maintained by a major global corporate insurance carrier based on input they collected from more than 2,700 risk management experts representing small, mid-size, and large corporations, the top 10 risks potentially faced by all companies in order of priority are:

1. Business interruption, including supply chain disruption
2. Health and workforce issues or limitations (including residual issues caused by the pandemic)
3. Cyber incidents, including information technology failures, outages, and data breaches
4. Market developments, including market fluctuations, volatility, and intensified competition
5. Changes in regulation and legislation, including tariffs and taxes
6. Natural catastrophes, including storms and flooding
7. Fire and explosion
8. Macroeconomic developments, including changes in monetary policy, inflation, and deflation
9. Climate change, including increased weather volatility
10. Political risks, including civil commotion and looting[3]

As is suggested by our enrichment scale, just envisioning the possibilities for improvement or anticipating risks is not sufficient; rather, if the company is committed to enhancing itself—to delivering better products, maintaining a satisfied workforce, meeting (and exceeding) customer expectations—the company has to set its full complement of resources in motion.

Marshaling the Resources

Effective teams do not occur naturally; they are a function of careful team member selection complemented by a common application of the protocols and mechanics of group interaction and decision making. In contrast, as we discussed in the Introduction, the statistic-based improvement methodologies—for example, operations research and Six Sigma—are generally minimally reliant on opinions and experience, preferring instead to rely extensively on computational analysis. Lean Manufacturing, which makes the team a centerpiece of its approach, expects teams to be high performing, but little guidance, if at all, is provided in regards to team member selection—instead deferring largely to a self-selection process or volunteer basis. And, although there is a standard decision-making methodology in Lean Manufacturing centered around reworking process flowcharts, interaction among team members is only guided by a set of generalized set of behaviors for maintaining order and decorum:

- Everyone shares responsibilities.
- Relaxed, cooperative atmosphere.
- Everyone involves/contributes according to their strengths/ abilities.
- Members understand and trust each other.
- Good listening: ideas listened to and developed.
- Members not frightened to contribute: no ridicule for failure.

The problem with this approach is that the team may or may not have the appropriate collective expertise or perspective and may not, despite the desired behaviors, have the degree of interaction, analytical attention, or deliberative process to arrive at optimum decisions. Moreover, whereas self-selection may be a reasonable strategy when considering a single process in isolation as the focus of the team's efforts, it cannot suffice when the intended scope of the team is to explore a much broader range of company implications.

In that instance, there are three factors that are the scaffolding of the team's success: (1) a disciplined process for the selection of appropriate team members, (2) a practical and systematically applied approach to arriving at decisions and recommendations, and (3) a formal method for recording the initial set of potential enrichment opportunities. The first two of these factors we will discuss here; the third factor (capturing enrichment opportunities) will be addressed in the next chapter.

Securing an Effective Team Culture

There are three primary attributes that determine a candidate's likelihood of being a solid contributor to a team: (1) commitment, (2) knowledge, and (3) reasonableness. Even when prospective team members nominate themselves or are identified by management or by their co-workers, each of these three attributes must be thoughtfully evaluated before the individual is accepted onto the team.

Commitment: Gaging commitment is not simply a matter of asking individuals how enthusiastic they are about supporting a particular team effort. The measure is equally a function of commitment to the project and commitment to the team—the degree of connectiveness one establishes with the group. It is, as social psychologists refer to it, a measure of ability to integrate within and foster a particular "social identity."

In one illuminating study of how social identity translates into promoting a community of support, two British psychologists studied the impact when people perceive themselves as having a shared, social identity. University students known to be vehement Manchester United fans (one of the premiere U.K. football teams) were selected as test subjects. In the process of walking across campus, each of these individuals witnessed a student trip and appear to be injured. Part of the research team, the supposedly injured students each wore one of three jerseys: (1) Manchester United, (2) Liverpool FC (a long-time, deeply reviled rival of Manchester United), or (3) plain, unadorned jerseys. Having observed the accident, the test subjects offered assistance to fellow Manchester United fans 80 percent of the time; offered assistance 70 percent of the time to Liverpool FC supporters; and only offered assistance 20 percent of the time to individuals who were seen as not being football enthusiasts.

The conclusion evident from the study was that the greater the degree of perceived community or shared social identity—the more exclusive and more tightly bounded the relationship—the more likely people are actively to engage in cooperative and mutually supportive behaviors.[4]

Unfortunately, in advance of chartering a company improvement team, there is no equivalent test to that as was applied to the university students. No yardstick exists by which to measure the degree to which a particular individual will likely bond with and become a contributing member of a community or team.

However, there are four factors that psychologists have identified that correlate with achieving a social identity (or sense of community) among team members. These four considerations, which can be assessed through discussions with prospective team members, consider the individual's motivation for participating in the group.

Expressed in the language of social psychologists, these four motivations linked to an understanding of team effort are:

- Egotism: The motivation is to support the group as a means of benefitting oneself.
- Altruism: The motivation is to support other individuals (who may or may not be team members).
- Collectivism: The motivation is to improve the circumstances of an entire group or population.
- Principlism: The motivation is to advance a tenet or ethic.[5]

Clearly, given the complexities of circumstance and personal history that underlie an individual's motivations, the four forms of motivation do not necessarily exist totally independent of one another; rather, any number of permutations can exist, further differentiated by the relative strengths of the motivating forces underpinning an individual's decisions and actions. As example, one can have primarily self-interests at heart (egotism), be a strong proponent of a group's effort (collectivism), and, at the same time, although perhaps at a less intense level, envision oneself as promoting a grander moral ethos (principlism). Nor, with limited exceptions, are any of the four types of motivation necessarily better or worse than another.

Using our Manchester United test subjects as example, each student's actions might have been influenced by any combination of motivating factors; moreover, even if multiple students were motivated by a similar slate of factors, there may still be differences in the factors' relative dominance and strength. Only through interviews can it be determined with certainty what motivations precipitated the students' responses:

Egotistical: Did they assist the injured student thinking they would earn some meritorious recognition and personal acknowledgment?

Altruism: Did they simply see there was a need to assist and stepped forward?

Collectivism: Did they perceive some common good inherent in the act?

Principlism: Did they, consequent to values inculcated in their upbringing, act in the belief that helping others was their moral obligation?

Even though there is not necessarily anything innately wrong with team members driven by egotistical or altruistic motives, enriching a company calls for a team whose primary motivations lie with collectivism and principlism—a commitment to advancing the performance of the team and the sustainability of the company.

Recognizing the role of motivation in achieving social identity and ultimate team success is the first step. The second step—which we will discuss presently after reviewing the other two characteristics defining team culture—is the means by which we can gauge—at least in a relative sense—a prospective team member's degree of commitment.

Knowledge: Knowledge of the system, process, or program under examination is the most common attribute used in selecting team members—whether engaged in Lean Manufacturing or using some less formal approach to improving performance. However, a common mistake is that in most instances sufficient knowledge is assumed to be available to the team if the team is composed of the "owner" of the subject systems complemented by employees with experience operating the system.

A limited band of expertise like this may be sufficient when the field of vision is purposely restricted. However, that same degree of expertise and experience will not work effectively when considering the broader horizon of company enrichment. In that instance, the team membership is not well served by a narrow focus or a limited sphere of expertise and experience, but, rather, relies on forging a team whose collective knowledge has substantial depth and breadth.

That depth and breadth requires substantive knowledge of seven, specific categories of information:

- Basic description of the process/system/program: How exactly does it operate, what are the inputs and outputs, what metrics exist that monitor performance, and what types of training or expertise is required for its safe and effective operation?
- Interfaces: How many systems or processes up- or downstream of the one being addressed rely on it for inputs, outputs, data, or products? How complex are those interfaces? Recognizing that interfaces within engineered systems are the points most susceptible to difficulties, how many times and in what manner has this system adversely affected other company operations? Are there supply lines susceptible to disruption?
- Requirements and regulations: What specific externally originated requirements control aspects of the system—controls on how it is designed, how it operates, limitations on production, and performance or quality standards?
- Company controls: How complex and rigid are company policies and procedures? What degree of local or operator decision making is allowed or required? How many documented instances of procedural violations have occurred in the recent past? How frequently have procedure and policy revisions been required?
- Attitudes and opinions: What is the predominant worker impression of the system—excellent, needs overhaul, is performing above or below par, is dangerous to operate?
- Receptiveness to improvement: Have there been previous improvement initiatives, and, if so, how have they been received by management? Were they implemented in an expedient manner, delayed, or never implemented? Were there

concerns about the cost or schedule impacts from the change? Did the changes, as implemented, substantially change or improve the system performance?

- Documentation: How current and accurate are the drawings, schematics, and procedures? Has the documentation kept pace with changes in how business is done and with the configuration of equipment?

Only when the team collectively has knowledge of these factors, or has immediate access to relevant information, is it prepared to conduct the quality of assessment that underpins a knowledge-driven evaluation and improvement. This knowledge is also critical in supporting a phased and disciplined process of analysis, including formulation of recommendations and their implementation (Table 1.3).

Reasonableness: Some concepts originate in a very informal circumstance only to become the foundational elements of a greater ethic. This is the evolution by which "reasonableness" became a predicate of the legal standard of care and has also come to be recognized as a cornerstone of a healthy team culture. In a famous case of libel and perjury (Tichborne Claimant 1871), the junior counsel for the defendant supposedly suggested that to be impartial, the court needed not to concentrate on the responses of the so-called experts but rather they should rely on the common man, the individual the attorney identified as "the man on the Clapham bus." Twenty-three years later, this metaphor was popularized in the analysis of the *English Constitution* authored by the journalist, Walter Bagehot who, as noted by the quotation heading this chapter, turned this hypothetical "bald-headed" bus rider into a metaphor for the common man.

Only a decade after that reference, the representation of reasonableness became a fixture in tort law. Defending counsel in the 1903 case of *McQuire v Western Morning News* (another liable case) concluded his comments by confronting the jury with the following challenge: "We must ask ourselves what the man on the Clapham omnibus would think."[6]

Thereby entrenched, the conjured image of an average man riding on his way to work in a horse-drawn bus between the English towns of Knightsbridge and Clapham became the institutionalized representation

Table 1.3 Knowledge-driven analysis

Operational Phase	Example of Opportunity Addressed	Typical Evaluation Criteria
Execution	Need for an integrating operational framework	• All processes aligned to strategic business imperatives • Tailored approach predicated on risks/process gaps/business sensitivity • Structure enhances operating perspective
	Need for improved timeliness and effectiveness of implementation	• Increased accountability for implementation • Resource allocation aligned with accountability for delivery of improvements • Better prioritization of efforts • Management engagement amplified implementation efforts appropriately integrated
Oversight	Need for a common basis for gauging suitability of processes and performance	• Industry standards used as basis for developing and assessing the quality of controls • Where available, industry-wide metrics used—to develop site-level and facility-level measures
	More rigorous oversight required	• Monthly reporting instituted • Structure establishes more effective working relationship within spectrum of interrelated processes • Management reviews added to monitor performance against goals
Improvement	Need to integrate a sustained continuous improvement program into the management control process	• Routine analyses form primary foundation for improvements • Integrated plans developed contributing to functional and topic area action plans • Change control process introduced

of the measure of normative behaviors. This is true whether applied to cases of negligence as is common in legal settings, impaneling members on a jury, or, as in our case, when selecting team members.

The reasonable man standard has several functions. . . . [It] promotes . . . balance [between individual and society] by assuming an allegedly objective and neutral standard by which to measure competing interests. . . . [The] reasonable man has an important function in epitomizing the acceptable citizen and providing a consistent and yet flexible model against which conduct can be measured. . . . The provision of a standardized abstract notion removes the need to set down detailed guidelines. . . . for every major kind of . . . conduct.[7]

From a legal perspective, defining the degree of reasonableness is a function of five elements. For our purposes, we have found that each of these five determinants of reasonableness as applied in legal contexts is immediately applicable to use in selecting our team members. As in any team, we are asking individuals for a reasonable, impartial, and candid interpretation of the facts and circumstances. In other words, the same reasonableness applied in standard of care cases (assessments of negligence) must be practiced by the team. When considered from this vantage point, reasonableness is readily understood as a natural and necessary complement to the other components of effective team culture: commitment and knowledge.

Each of these factors used to gage the appropriateness of standard of care (or due diligence practiced by the team) is summarized below and accompanied by a single example of a circumstance that could have various interpretations were not the matter subjected to careful analysis and reasoned judgment.

1. *Foreseeability*: Should the individual have anticipated the likelihood or consequence of actions or inaction? Example: instituting a change in business strategy contrary to market indicators that results in reduced market share and inability to raise investment capital. Is this action reasonable or unreasonable?

2. *Magnitude of risk*: Should the individual have recognized the full import of the consequences of an action or inaction? Example: introducing new hazardous materials or chemicals into a process and assuming worker training previously received by the staff will be adequate. Is this action reasonable or unreasonable?

3. *Social utility*: Can the actions or inactions be understood as an effort to benefit a community or group. Example: initiating investment actions intending to save workers' pensions, but instead resulting in plant shutdowns. Was this action reasonable or unreasonable?

4. *Practicality of precautions*: How appropriate were the controls as established and implemented? Example: instituting extensive training, publishing new administrative controls, and constructing expensive engineered barriers costing millions to upgrade a process that historically has had the best safety record of any company function. Is this action reasonable or unreasonable?

5. *Common practice*: Are the actions or inactions the same as would have been taken by other similarly qualified individuals? Example: dismissing the machine operator who shut down the entire production process, costing the company a major client, because she thought she observed a potentially serious safety risk. Is this action reasonable or unreasonable?

Taking a Disciplined Approach to Selecting Team Members

The initial selection. Selecting team members and targeting individuals with the right attitudes and behaviors is not significantly different from the two other common activities involving selecting individuals: employment interviews and the process of voir dire used when impaneling juries. Although generally focused most acutely on the interviewee's knowledge, both selection processes have reason to gauge commitment and reasonableness.

In an employment interview, the objective is to identify the candidate who has the right expertise and experience to meet specific needs—current or anticipated—by the company and who will fit in well with the company culture and with fellow employees. Impaneling jurors—which looks to identify people whose opinions, perspectives, and experiences align with the themes of argument the attorneys intend to present during a trial—is particularly informing and supporting of considering all three factors (knowledge, commitment, and reasonableness).

Selecting jurors, as practiced in early American trials, was largely a function of identifying individuals who, based on their familiarity with the matter being litigated, would testify as to their personal knowledge of the facts of the case and their knowledge of the character of the litigants. Clearly this approach favored an individual's knowledge over concern for the individual's reasonableness or for the witness' commitment to the integrity of the proceedings.

Over time, the procedure was totally redefined: Rather than seating a jury based on their knowledge of the facts, the objective (as we now experience it) became the selection of individuals who were in great measure ignorant of the facts and unacquainted with any of the parties involved in the legal matter. Ostensibly, this change was introduced primarily as a consequence of the expanding role of the courts in resolving legal disputes, which in turn made it increasingly more difficult to find jurors acquainted with aspects of the trial. It was, for all intents and purposes, a shift away from valuing knowledge to the exclusion of reasonableness and commitment to a valuing of reasonableness and commitment over knowledge.

One immediate need fostered by this shift in orientation was the attorneys' need to gather sufficient information about prospective jurors to allow them to determine who to seat in the jury box—trying to mask juror choices of benefit to themselves while also uncovering candidates they might choose to "strike."

The principal means by which this information is obtained is with a jury questionnaire. As succinctly noted in one review of the use of jury questionnaires: "Courts increasingly rely on jury questionnaires for two purposes. First, questionnaires are used to qualify jurors for jury service. Second, they are used to obtain information about jurors for jury selection."[8]

Rather than simply accepting candidates, we use this same principle in selecting prospective team members. Our approach is a two-step process: (1) Using interviews, we select potential candidates from among the complete slate of proposed candidates; (2) we determine which subset of candidates identified in Step 1, once assembled on a team, would best encompass the cultural and behavioral characteristics necessary to achieve the results we are after.

Step 1. Down-selecting the candidate list: As we had described previously, there are three elements of a successful team culture: commitment, knowledge, and reasonableness. Unlike many team improvement initiatives that assume only knowledge is a predicate of success—as is demonstrated in the ways in which both Lean Manufacturing and Six Sigma identify their teams—we look to ensure a balance of these three factors.

Only with a balance of the three cultural elements is there a high probability of innovative change and also opportunity to employ the same group of people in expanding enrichment efforts into other processes, company systems, and strategies. As we have learned, having knowledge without commitment and reasonableness is a formula for loose alignment of team personnel and a likelihood of essentially repeating—or defaulting to—much of the existing corporate practices and strategy. Minimizing knowledge, on the other hand, introduces the probability that the team's achievements will be limited and narrowly focused. Although the three cultural dimensions do not need to be equally strong, there needs to be sufficient balance among them so that the full benefit of the team's resources (i.e., all three cultural attributes) are concentrated on achieving optimal results (Figure 1.3).

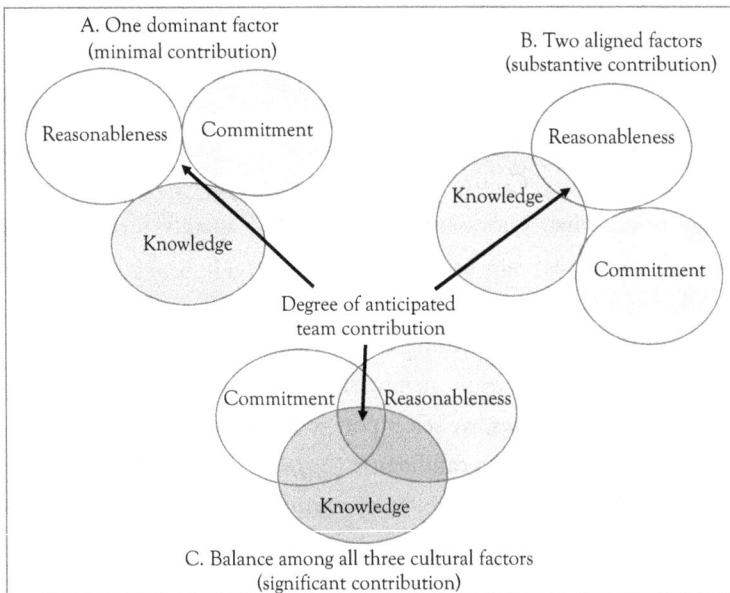

A. One dominant factor (minimal contribution)

Reasonableness   Commitment

Knowledge

B. Two aligned factors (substantive contribution)

Reasonableness

Knowledge

Commitment

Degree of anticipated team contribution

Commitment   Reasonableness

Knowledge

C. Balance among all three cultural factors (significant contribution)

Figure 1.3 Maintaining a cultural balance

At the same time, the team dynamic needs to encompass a range of behaviors that complement the cultural elements. Although any number of studies can be considered when determining an effective set of leadership attributes, we have found that the principles employed by Amazon are most immediately conducive to promoting the caliber of team engagement we are seeking. It has the right value set and is a model team members can readily identify as representative of the formula underpinning one of the most successful and innovative companies (Table 1.4).[9]

To deliver a team with these cultural and behavioral characteristics, we use a questionnaire that solicits discussion intending to reveal the individual's disposition. In an informal setting, and over the course of 30 to 60 minutes, we meet individually with each candidate. The questions we ask are not intended as a fixed script but serve as the set of themes to be reviewed with every candidate. Consistent with what has been learned in the process of questioning jurors (or as is typically delineated on a prospective candidate's resume), we begin with discussing

Table 1.4 Amazon's 14 principles of leadership

Principle	Team Application
Be customer obsessed	Ensure customers are completely satisfied
Take ownership	Lead by example; emphasize the group over self-interest
Invent and simplify	Advocate for innovative approaches, techniques, and strategies
Have good judgment	Acknowledge good ideas and proposals when they are presented
Learn and be curious	Stay inquisitive; stay informed
Develop the best	Strengthen each team member and make them successful
Insist on high standards	Set high expectations and facilitate their achievement
Think big	Inspire the team to work harder and deliver more
Act rapidly	Be decisive; promote a bias for action
Use resources wisely	Maximize team resources; minimize impacts of constraints and limits beyond team control
Earn trust	Support and encourage each individual's efforts
Dive deep	Pay attention to the details
Have backbone	Challenge and, as appropriate, displace the status quo
Deliver results	Use the collective strength of the team to overcome challenges that impede progress or fulfillment of commitments

basic details about the individual's experience and background; this opening exchange best serves to establish an informal, conversational tone for the interview (Table 1.5).

Table 1.5 *Team selection questionnaire*

Process Team:		Prospective Team Member:				
Question		Potential Level of Contribution				
		Significant	Major	Minor	Limited	None
1	Do you have experience with this process?					
2	What is your opinion of the process?					
3	What aspects of the process are most in need of improvement?					
4	Have you worked on inputs or outputs of this process?					
5	Has the process had past issues and, if so, how (and how effectively) were they addressed?					
6	Do you have other training or experience that will advance the team's efforts?					
7	How will you respond if the team does not agree with your ideas, points, or conclusions?					
8	What would it take to change your mind?					
9	Why do you want to be on this team?					
10	Are there individuals or organizations you think need to be on (or not be on) the team?					
11	How do you and the company benefit from improving the performance of this process?					

12	How would you define team success/team failure?					
13	Are there limitations on your time or availability to support the team's efforts?					
14	How do you think management will receive our recommendations (and how likely are they to be implemented)?					
15	Are there other processes you think the team should tackle next?					
16	Do you expect this effort to lead to other enhancements in company business (e.g., training, strategies)?					
17	Are there any reasons you should be on this team that we haven't discussed?					
Scoring						
Cultural contribution quotient (boxes checked)	X5 =	X4 =	X3 =	X2 =	X1 =
Leadership potential as suggested by interview	X3 =	X2 =	X2 =	X1 =	X1 =
Total team contribution anticipated						

Once the individual interviews have been completed, we discuss the scores and review the individuals who had received the highest ratings. From this subset of prospective team candidates, we determine which combination of candidates is most likely to provide a balance among the three cultural components and also will foster the right team temperament.

In general, the intent is to identify a group of individuals who collectively represent the highest potential for contributing to the team effort and achieving success. To this end, our interviews and the ultimate team selection highlight the nine questions specifically designed to elicit discussion on the subjects of commitment, knowledge, and reasonableness (Table 1.6).

Table 1.6 Scores required for fielding an effective team

Team Selection			
Process Team:	Membership:		
Question		Anticipated Contribution	
		Significant	Major
1	What experience do you have working with this process?	Knowledge	
2	What is your opinion of how well the process works?		Reasonableness
6	Do you have other training or experience that will advance the team's efforts?		Knowledge
7	How will you respond if the team does not agree with your ideas, points of view, conclusions, or recommendations?	Reasonable-ness	
8	What would it take to convince you to change your mind?		Reasonableness
9	Why do you want to be on this team?	Commitment	
12	How would you define team success/team failure?		Commitment
13	Are there limitations on your time or availability to support the team's efforts?	Commitment	
16	Do you see this effort as leading potentially to broader enhancements in how the company does business (e.g., training, organizational structure, strategies)?		Knowledge

As is evident, this final selection step is in large measure a subjective exercise. Nonetheless, the process of using a structured interview with the express objective of fielding a team with the right attributes to drive for and deliver substantive results is a great deal more likely to succeed than a team randomly selected or one that does not inherently comprise the necessary predicates of success.

The next step, having assembled a team, is to establish a common methodology for team decision making.

Instituting a Formal Approach to Decision Making

Recognizing the Potential Pitfalls in Team Decision Making

Returning momentarily to the Challenger and the shortcomings of a highly knowledgeable, committed, and (presumably) reasonable team provides a strong rationale not only for expending significant effort in the selection of team members but also in ensuring an efficient and effective method by which to reach team decisions.

The Challenger accident resulted because the team failed to discern that launch temperature could contribute to O-ring failure (i.e., not that the temperature definitely would cause failure, just that failure was a possibility). As the commission reviewing the Challenger accident determined, the engineers' time-driven efforts to reach unanimity had led to a narrowing of critical analysis.

This refocusing on unanimity over depth of analysis or unanimity displacing reason is a team condition known as "Groupthink." As was demonstrated in the case of the Challenger accident, Groupthink—a term coined in 1972 by Yale psychologist Irving Janis—can entail a range of confirmation biases that redirect and, potentially, diminish the suitability and applicability of team decisions and recommendations. Among the most common biases contributing to Groupthink are the following eight, all of which were exhibited in the case of the Challenger:

1. *Invulnerability*: A bias that leads teams to be overly optimistic and willing to accept rather than thoroughly assess risks. NASA's 20+-year string of 55 successful missions, including having landed astronauts on the moon and having launched Skylab, contributed to NASA accepting ostensibly minor deviations in conditions (i.e., launch temperature) as acceptable risks.

2. *Rationalization*: In this bias, the team develops arguments to dismiss or minimize warnings, risks, and alternative interpretations of information. Despite the fact that evidence of potential O-ring failure was introduced during the conversation among the engineers, flight center personnel dismissed the assertions as lacking sufficient proof. Rather than ensuring the launch was safe, the team, as one engineer

noted during the commission hearing, had totally inverted their purpose: Instead of determining whether the flight was absolutely safe,
they placed the burden on the engineers in the minority to prove it
was definitely unsafe.

> This was a meeting where the determination was to launch
> and it was up to us to prove beyond a shadow of a doubt that
> it was *not* safe to do so. This is in total reverse to what the
> position usually is in a preflight . . . readiness review.

3. *Stereotyped view of others*: Differing opinions may be dismissed
   because the individual offering the opinion is not respected. Several
   NASA officials, assuming they knew best, acted as if the contract
   engineers' opinions were uninformed and, therefore, not worthy of
   substantive evaluation.
4. *Pressure on dissent*: A majority of the team may begin to pressure
   those with dissenting opinions to change their minds. Bullying
   by the NASA officials, the pressure on the dissenters to prove their
   assertions—claims that could not be proven without further testing—
   eventually led the dissenting engineers to concede their analysis was
   "inconclusive."
5. *Self-censorship*: Team members begin to drop or minimize their dissenting positions, not because they are convinced the opinions are
   invalid, but in the interests of advancing team harmony. Following
   the concession that the temperature issue was inconclusive, the principal dissenting engineer not only withdrew his position but also
   provided written statement to NASA that he was now in agreement
   to launch.
6. *Illusion of unanimity*: Rather than explore alternate positions, members of the majority continue to provide evidence reinforcing their
   position; dissenting team members remain silent. There was never a
   full accounting of each engineer's stance regarding potential O-ring
   failure. Moreover, not a single NASA engineer offered any support
   for the contractor's concern or for the need for further research.
7. *Mindguarding*: Information that might undermine the majority
   position or discredit their interpretation of the facts is withheld.

During the Challenger discussion, a history of problems and design changes indirectly related to the O-rings was withheld. Although the withheld information would not have conclusively validated a potential O-ring failure, it would have more strenuously argued for a decision to delay launch pending further analysis.

8. *Morality*: A team member may believe, without question, in a principle or ethic strongly enough to override concern for the potential consequences of actions taken or not taken. One manager who tried to gain support to stop the launch stated during the course of the evening's discussions that if something went wrong, he didn't "want to have to be the person to stand up in front of a board of inquiry and say I went ahead and told them to go ahead and fly this thing."[10]

Battling the Biases

As we noted, the consequences of allowing biases such as those experienced in Groupthink are threefold: (1) incomplete analysis of the alternatives, (2) loss of focus on the objectives, and (3) failure to thoroughly examine risks. Creating a process that protects against such confirmatory biases rests with team behaviors and the role of the team leader (or team facilitator).

At the beginning of the first team session, we review our 10 rules for effective teams—rules that focus not so much on maintaining decorum, but rather on promoting an engaged analysis of the information, the alternatives, and the risks, complemented by thoughtful evaluation of the feasibility, completeness, and practicality of proposed recommendations and conclusions:

1. Always act in the best interests of the organization you represent, your team, and your company.
2. Bring your experience, expertise, and your judgment to every meeting.
3. Be assertive, but not to the exclusion of listening carefully.
4. Acknowledge sound ideas and valid opinions—even if they differ or conflict with your own.
5. Follow the data; rely on information—maintaining a balance between the bigger picture and the fine details.

6. Don't settle; always strive for the optimum answer.

7. Encourage engagement by all team members.

8. Understand and address the challenges and the obstacles.

9. Measure success by what the customer gains, not by team satisfaction.

10. Never lose focus of the team's goals.

These behaviors and expectations do not occur without a team lead or facilitator who is prepared to hold the team accountable. Most significant is that the team lead is an equal partner with the rest of the team, charged with monitoring and challenging the team when it deviates from the path to success, is exhibiting the effects of confirmatory bias, or is concluding prematurely before an issue or topic has been sufficiently examined. Having the team lead act as a participating member of the team substantively strengthens the team performance by adding one more voice and also ensures that the focus remains on achieving results, not being driven—as is often the case with facilitated sessions—primarily by the clock, a schedule, or an agenda.

Yet, recognizing biases and having established an expected suite of behaviors and team expectations only represent two of the three legs of the preparation. The final component is arming the team with a methodology that not only encourages debate but also provides a tangible means to diagnose the efficacy of arguments being presented.

The Decision-Making Process

All too often, it is assumed that simply articulating the problem to be addressed and then relying on the team's natural inclinations is sufficient to ensure that the right conclusions will be reached and effective recommendations will result. When this attitude prevails, the team is encouraged to use simple recordings of their ideas (e.g., flowcharts) as the sole or primary vehicle for arriving at decisions.

Our approach, in contrast, is based on a hybrid we developed of three strategies of effective argumentation—not decision making. All the patterns of decision making as summarized in Table 1.7 rely, to varying

Table 1.7 *Commonly applied approaches to decision making*

Scientific Method	Engineering Method	Design Process	Business Process	Standard Process	Six Sigma
• Develop hypothesis • Define experiment • Conduct experiment • Analyze results • Compare results with hypothesis • Refine hypothesis • Redo experiments	• Conduct preliminary analysis • Refine issues • Conduct design activities (e.g., conceptual design) • Select option(s) • Conduct final design activities • Initiate project • Monitor versus plan	• Analysis • Synthesis • Evaluation • Decision • Optimization • Revision	• Think • Plan • Do • Check • Revise	• Define the problem • Analyze the problem • Establish goals and objectives • Select the best solution • Implement	• Define the problem • Measure • Analyze • Improve • Control

degrees, on the assumption that an innate and naturally occurring synthesis will occur within the team, assuring the integrity of the process, the correctness of the conclusions, and the appropriateness of the recommendations promulgated.

That belief is, in itself, a variation of the illusion of unanimity. No properly constructed team—one with diverse perspectives, experience, and expertise—is immune from unintended biases as it progresses through the decision-making process.

Recognizing this vulnerability, our approach is to equip the team with a decision-making methodology based on synthesizing elements from three major theories of argument—classical, Rogerian, and the approach developed in Stephen Toulmin's *The Uses of Argument*. Integrating these three approaches provides a process that is conducive to promoting careful analysis; maintaining the cohesiveness of the team; and producing credible, reliable, and optimal recommendations for improvements—whether examining company processes, technology, personnel performance, governance, or strategy.

Integrating these approaches to argument (the elements of which are summarized in Table 1.8) provides the team with three critical dimensions for effective decision making:

- A decision-oriented structure of argument predicated on reasoning and formal, syllogistic logic
- A nonconfrontational structure of argument focused on promoting common ground
- An evidence-based structure of argument focused both on depth of assertion and on refutation.

Cicero, a contemporary of Julius Caesar, recorded in *De Inventione* (85 BCE) the five canons or tenets of rhetoric, a structure used in the preparation of hundreds of speeches he delivered before the Roman people and the Roman Senate. These canons represent the approach passed down essentially unaltered through centuries of rhetorical theory. It is a process that proceeds from gaining the audience's attention, through a substantive and structured argument of the facts and reasoning, concluding with statement of actions needed.

Carl Rogers, a psychologist at the University of Chicago and one of the founders of "Humanistic Psychology," proposed an alternative orientation regarding argument:

I would like to propose as an hypothesis . . . that the major barrier to mutual interpersonal communication is our very natural tendency to judge, to evaluate, to approve or disapprove, the statement of the other person, or the other group.

To avoid this tendency, Rogers suggested people need to

listen with understanding. . . . to see the expressed idea and attitude from the other person's point of view, to sense how it feels to him, to achieve his frame of reference in regard to the thing he is talking about.

As one means of accomplishing this "listening with understanding," Rogers proposed a very challenging approach to communication: "each

Table 1.8 *The three utilized theories of rhetoric*

	Classical Oration	Rogerian Argument	Toulmin Model
Source	Cicero, *De Inventione*	Carl Rogers, "Communication: Its Blocking and Its Facilitation"	Stephen Toulmin, *The Uses of Argument*
Overview	A decision-oriented structure of argument predicated on reasoning and formal, syllogistic logic	A nonconfrontational structure of argument focused on promoting common ground	An evidence-based structure of argument focused both on depth of assertion and on refutation
Methodology	• *Exordium* (Introduction): Gain the audience's attention and introduce the topic • *Narratio* (Background): Supply sufficient context to understand the case • *Partitio* (Proposition): State the claim or thesis, key issues, and outline the major points of the argument that will follow • *Confirmatio* (Proof): Detail the assumptions and provide the reasoning, subclaims, and evidence • *Refutatio* (Refutation): Anticipate and refute the opposing argument, demonstrating that you have a sound basis for dismissing the opponent's reasoning and conclusions • *Peroratio* (Call to Action): Summarize your position and explain what needs to be done, actions taken	• Introduction: Identify the problem you intend to solve, offering the opportunity for change • Opposing views: In an accurate and neutral manner, present the opposing view, with an eye to demonstrating that you are willing to consider an opposing view • Understanding: Explain the positive implications of the opposing view, but also make clear its limitations/limits • Position statement: Explain your position, including the evidence, assumptions, and reasoning • Statement of context: Explain the limitations and appropriate application of your conclusions and evidence • Statement of compromise: Appeal to the opposition to the opposition by showing the benefit of your position (and perhaps) the opportunity for compromise	• Claim: State the conclusion whose merits you plan to establish • Data/grounds: Provide the facts, assumptions, and evidence that demonstrate the validity and appropriateness of the claims • Warrant: Establish the chain of reasoning that demonstrates the association between the grounds and the claim • Backing: Offer additional support (reasoning, evidence, assumptions, justifications) that substantiate the warrant • Qualifiers: Characterize the strength of the claim, warrant, and backing • Rebuttal: Demonstrate the knowledge and weakness (inappropriateness) of the counter arguments

person can speak up for himself after he has first restated the ideas and feelings of the previous speaker accurately, and to that speaker's satisfaction."[11]

Complementing the classical approach and Rogers' strategy for building common ground, we introduce the team to the work of Stephen Toulmin, a British philosopher. His methodology is provided as a means not only to draw the evidence out, but also to allow the team to dissect and depict all the facets of the argument—the information, the underlying (and often tacit) reasoning and assumptions, the strength of the assertions, and the potential points of refutation.

Originally developed in Toulmin's efforts to define how to establish sound arguments when evaluating ethical or moral issues, his model for constructing and evaluating arguments was applied to basic rhetorical arguments in his 1958 text, *The Uses of Argument*.

For the purposes of promoting effective team analysis and communication, Toulmin's model offers two very significant enhancements. First of all, his approach not only provides insights into the principal claims being made, but also delves into the underlying assumptions—that is, the reasoning—underpinning the assertions. In so doing, the supporting bases are made evident as are the relative strengths, weaknesses, and possible refutations to the argument. Second, there is the visualization of the argument.

Somewhat analogous to diagramming sentences—the Kellogg method often taught in grade schools—Toulmin provided the template for depicting arguments. This template, which can be applied to arguments, whether simple or highly complex, gives all team members opportunity to assess each of the components of the argument, not just the claim that drives the argument. In so doing, implicit biases become immediately evident and can be specifically challenged and debated. As example, Figure 1.4 provides a simple illustration of the Toulmin model of argument.[12]

Obviously, stopping to build these depictions for every claim or argument raised during team discussions would prove onerous and extremely time consuming. Therefore, our approach is to use the pictorial breakdown in four very specific circumstances:

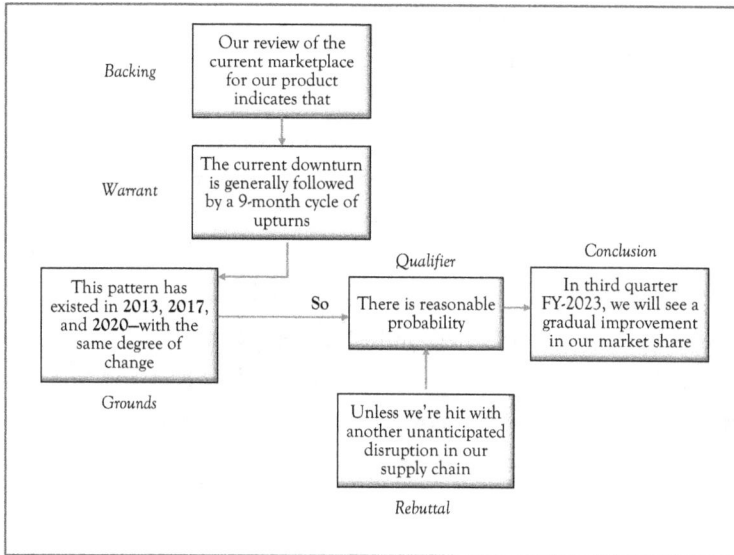

Figure 1.4 Sample illustration of Toulmin's model of argument

1. There is a disagreement among team members in regard to the adequacy or accuracy of assumptions.
2. A claim being made appears to have insufficient basis and the team needs to understand where and to what degree judgment and reason rather than fact need to be applied.
3. A claim being made appears to be reasonable but is not well understood by the team.
4. Final recommendations and conclusions are evaluated as the last step prior to their formal acceptance by the team to secure consensus and confirmation of the team's conclusions.

Putting the Team to Work

Integrating these three models of argument (classical, Rogerian, and the Toulmin display) into a single foundation for decision making is explained to the team members in our first session:

- Use the classical approach as the primary sequence for proceeding through the enrichment process.

- Use the predicates of Rogers' humanistic approach during discussions to promote team cohesion, consensus, and common ground.
- Use the Toulmin model of argument to guard against biases, analyze disputed or intuitive arguments, and validate final decisions and recommendations.

Now, with the proper team in place, with the protocols and behaviors for team discussions elaborated, and with an appreciation of the methods for conducting the arguments and for reaching their decisions, the team needs only an explanation of how all the pieces fit together.

That plan as we explain to the team is to proceed through a series of gates:

1. Sharing perspectives: getting an idea of everyone's initial thoughts, opinions, and relevant experience
2. Developing consensus: the analysis and synthesizing of the various perspectives
3. Securing commitment: firming up the arguments and reaching final consensus
4. Creating community of purpose: agreeing on the path forward (Figure 1.5)

Each gate may be a single meeting or a series of meetings; the team with assistance from the team lead decides when a gate or stage has been completed and when the team is ready to move forward.

Given this preparation, the team is now ready and equipped to deliver the full range of potential company enrichments: The team is now armed with the appropriate behaviors and protocols; aware of the biases and the means for defending against them; and provided with a strategy for stepping through a process that integrates the positive attributes of conducting the discussions and reaching decisions.

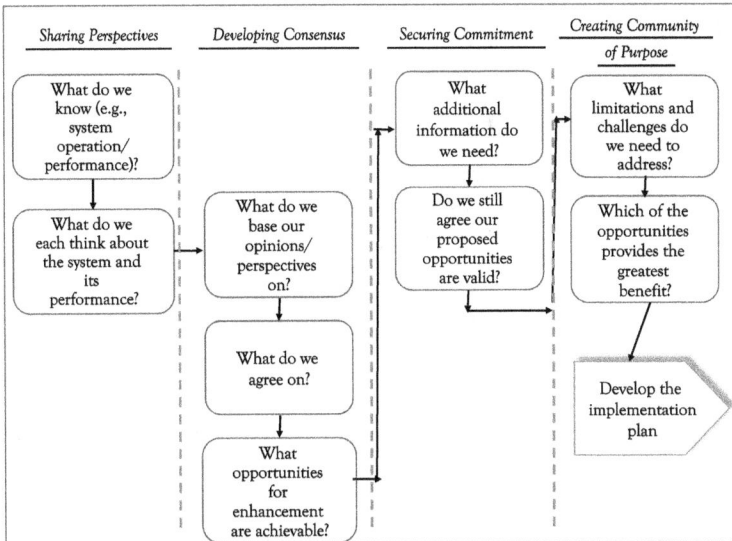

Figure 1.5 Basic enrichment process

In other words, the team is now ready to go to work!

CHAPTER 2

Building a Community of Purpose

The movements . . . are connected in all their parts. If errors have been committed, they ought to be corrected; if the policy is sound, it ought to be supported. It is by a thorough knowledge of the whole subject that [people] are enabled to judge correctly of the past and to give a proper direction to the future.

—President James Monroe
Second Inaugural Address, March 5, 1821

Colditz Castle, not far from Leipzig and Dresden, Germany, sits on a hilltop overlooking a tributary of the River Elbe some 300 feet below. Built originally in 1046 to be a royal hunting lodge and partially burned down some 60 years later, the castle has been reconstructed, modified, and used for a range of purposes over its history.

In the latter part of the 18th century, the castle served as a workhouse where indigent townspeople toiled in the tailor shop, the spinning rooms, and while maintaining castle grounds. The 19th century saw the castle converted to a State Institute for the Incurable Mentally Ill, a purpose it served through the first quarter of the 20th century. After a brief period of housing political prisoners, the castle resumed its role as a health center, but was tarnished by a record of mistreating patients and was abandoned.

The German military, inheriting this dark reputation and convinced that escape from the hilltop promontory would be impossible, began using the castle in 1940 as a prisoner of war camp—housing roughly 500 Allied officers. As one prisoner described: "Such a castle for enemies from a distant country struck the note of doom and was a sight that made the bravest quail."[1] Given its daunting façade, the castle was used exclusively for housing officers who at other camps had demonstrated their penchant for planning and executing escapes.

Escape certainly appeared improbable at Colditz. In addition to its remote location and the fact that the castle sits upon an outcrop of volcanic rock, walls were more than 6 feet thick; prisoners' cells encircled a courtyard, the only exit from which was blocked by three sets of guarded gates; and the number of guards posted at the castle essentially equaled the number of prisoners.

Nevertheless, prior to the prison's closing in 1945, there were 73 escape attempts; 22 officers succeeded in getting clear of the camp. "They were 'gone away' as it was termed."[2] Yet, two prisoners who didn't get away were part of perhaps the most ingenious escape plot ever conceived: Build a manned glider and then launch it from the castle roof!

Designed using plans outlined in a book from the prison library (*Airframes, Part II*), the glider was to be launched from the castle roof (a height of approximately 100 feet), catapulted by a bathtub filled with tons of concrete rubble excavated in a previous attempted tunneling escape. The tub—dropped approximately 60 feet through several cutaway sections in the castle floors—would transfer the downward force through a system of pulleys, propelling the glider. The thrust would send the glider, fitted with an automatic release hook, hurtling across the roof on a runway constructed of flat boards. Assuming success, the glider would sail two officers to freedom.

Of course, the imaginative scheme necessitated equally inspired strategies. While one prisoner delivered plans (including elevations and parts templates), another prisoner created tools—a minute saw, a side-framed saw, a square, a gauge, and three planes of varying length; in addition, a drill was obtained through bribery. Then, of course, was the challenge of parts for the glider.

All resources available to the prisoners were fair game: As example, the fuselage and main spar of the wing were made from floorboards; cotton prison sleeping bags provided "skinning" for the glider; the control wires were assembled from abandoned field telephone wires; and glue was obtained on the prison black market. But having the materials still left the matter of where to build the vehicle. That problem was solved by construction of a false wall sectioning off approximately a 10' × 30' portion of the top attic over the Castle Chapel.

As a modest test run, a toy-size model using the glider design, launched by one of the prisoners from a window above the castle courtyard, "glided beautifully," landing by the feet of one of the guards.[3] With the design documents in hand, tools and materials ready, and a work area established, glider construction began in earnest in May 1944 and was completed before the year's end. Launch was planned for spring 1945. However, before the glider could take flight, the war ended and the prisoners at Colditz Castle were liberated.[4]

Like the Delta Airlines fleet problem discussed in our Introduction, the process of building a glider and developing a launch capability to escape Colditz Castle represents a problem of significant complexity. However, unlike the computational analysis invoked in the airlines' analysis, the Colditz Castle escape plot was—by necessity—fashioned exclusively on the three facets of team culture we discussed in Chapter 1: knowledge, commitment, and reasonableness.

The plot also illuminates the accompanying focus that must attend team culture if process enhancement is to be sufficiently robust to serve as foundation for broader institutional enrichment. To advance the robustness and breadth of enrichment we are after, the attention paid to process must be accompanied by a similar depth of study regarding the impacts and implications of factors such as variables, constraints, and interfaces.

We will return to Colditz and what has been called "the Second World War's most audacious escape plan" momentarily, but first let's examine how this team culture and the associated examination of variations, constraints, and interfaces set the necessary framework for corporate enrichment.[5]

The Process for Improving Processes

As was mentioned at the conclusion of Chapter 1, the basic flow for assessing and enhancing processes is a four-step sequence:

1. Sharing perspectives
2. Developing consensus
3. Securing commitment
4. Creating a community of purpose

Sharing Perspectives

The initial work with the team is focused on establishing what is known and perceived relative to the process under consideration. At the most fundamental level, this initial analysis requires an appreciation of the general expectations for procedures and the systems that administer them.

Procedures and procedure systems are designed to achieve three primary roles:

1. Reflect the philosophy of operation that management imposes based on its corporate beliefs, culture, experience, and expectations.
2. Establish and maintain compliance with requirements (applicable laws, regulations, business standards, and accepted industry practices).
3. Fulfill any specific commitments made by management in response to direction from the board of directors, audits, oversight groups, and stakeholders (the public, local authorities, etc.).

To assist the team in fully evaluating a specific process, beyond recognizing the three summary objectives just cited, they need to know the expectations that govern procedure systems. As we have learned from many years administering procedure programs at major facilities in the United States and the United Kingdom (and as established in numerous industry standards), although procedures and procedure system designs differ from one company to the next (and even, at times, between functions within a company), to be effective, procedure programs must operate according to a dozen defining attributes (Table 2.1).

These management requirements translate the design requirements into the company's procedures. In so doing, they are intended to synthesize all the elements we have identified as candidate areas for potential enrichment: process, technology, training, governance, and strategy.

One side of this synthesis represents the bases for ensuring the final product captures and reflects attributes required to enable users to efficiently execute the procedures. The other side of this integration effort ensures the intent of commitments, requirements, and company strategies are woven into the process and done in a way so as not to impede the efficient completion of the tasks addressed by the procedure. In other

Table 2.1 Attributes of an effective procedure system

System Principle	Expectations
Policy exists for development of procedures	• Purposes and limitations of procedures are clearly established • The functions of the various company document types and their interrelationships are spelled out
Guidelines set policy for use of company document types	• Guidelines detail how procedures are used during normal and emergency (or off-normal) situations • Guidelines explain expectations of how procedure compliance is achieved, enforced, and documented
Authority and accountability defined	• Formal authorization and alignment are established for all contributing individuals and organizations • Sufficient resources are provided • Metrics or other assessment criteria are in place • A comprehensive description document is available
Integration among management systems enforced	• Implementation of regulations, commitments, and expectation is tracked across organizational boundaries to ensure work is coordinated and interfaces are efficient
Specific criteria exist detailing when procedures are required	• Routine assessments are conducted consistent with the frequency and complexity of the activity • Risks and vulnerabilities are evaluated • Compliance with quality and industry standards is enforced
Appropriate bases are defined when developing procedures	• Referenceable documentation is maintained • Process design is in keeping with company operating philosophy; technical and design bases; operating history; and lessons learned
Procedures are prepared consistent with the bases	• Appropriate interfaces are maintained along with shared availability of expertise • The process follows established development and design standards
Interdisciplinary reviews conducted	• Appropriate resources are provided • Review requirements and protocols are maintained
Verification of the content and validation of its usability are rigorously directed	• Appropriate personnel attest to the correctness, completeness, and usability of the procedure • Final verification is undertaken before first use • The validation method is consistent with the complexity of the process, risks, and operating experience • A single individual attests to the procedure's readiness for use
A disciplined revision process is provided	• Adequate controls ensure revision process does not lessen integrity of procedure • Periodic reviews conducted to ensure currency is retained
Access to the document is controlled	• Controlled distribution ensures personnel use the most current, approved version and have ease of access
Training is required	• All procedure users, authors, reviewers, and approvers trained

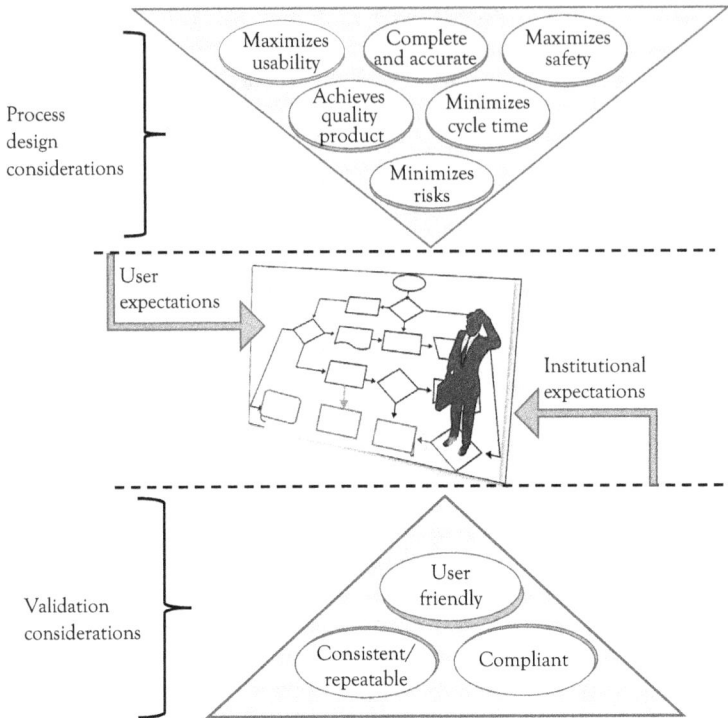

Figure 2.1 Basic procedural expectations

words, the technical and political aspects of the work must be aligned and reconciled with the capabilities, training, and expertise of the individuals charged with conducting the work (Figure 2.1).

Bringing these diverse elements into focus for the team begins with the basics of articulating and recording what they know and think about the process. The means by which these considerations are introduced is by segmenting the elements of the process and then engaging the team in discussion of the associated roles and responsibilities.

For illustrating purposes, let's assume the team is engaged in evaluating the process a large company is using for receipt control—the activities ensuring the company is buying only the materials and equipment it needs and is getting precisely what it is paying for. It is a process that begins when one of the company functions identifies an acquisition need and ends when the requested commodity has been validated as meeting the designated specifications, is determined to be in suitable condition for use, and then is released to the requesting organization.

The first step in defining an effective and efficient receipt control process, as shown in Table 2.2, is to create a matrix that lists the major segments of the process—from beginning to end (as described above), and to list all organizations and functions within the company that contribute (directly or indirectly) to completion of any of the process segments.

Once the team has agreed that the segmenting is appropriate and all players have been identified, it's time to start filling in the specific activities, responsibilities, and functions each organization plays. In some cases, an organization may only have a single cell in the responsibilities matrix that applies to them. In other cases, an organization may have an entry in every column. As an example of the process, Table 2.3 highlights a single row, the role played by the Engineering department in the receipt control process. (Certain columns from Table 2.2 where Engineering has no role have been eliminated for purposes of this illustration.)

Completing the matrix is an iterative process. Often, it is not until team members read an updated version that they find that an entry from another department spurs additional material they need to add to their own row. At other times, the process requires some assistance. This is the point at which the team lead asks questions to provoke additional input or to resolve gaps or inconsistencies.

Being that our goal is to treat these inquiries as discussions, we have learned that the best means to keep track of issues that needed clarification subsequent to the initial drafting of the matrix is to have a recording device separate from the responsibilities table. As shown in Table 2.4, we use a three-column format that indicates the original statement, what clarification was needed, and the clarification as agreed upon.

Once the team agrees all gaps have been sufficiently addressed, the appropriate adjustment is made to the responsibility table, which then goes through another cycle of reviews. As is the case with filling in the responsibility table, this process of soliciting clarifications also often results in several iterations before the team is satisfied and ready to move on to the next stage of the process.

Table 2.2 Process table indicating contributing organizations

	Identify Procurement Need	Identify Controls	Complete Requisition Process	Receive Procured Item	Provide Storage	Conduct Receipt Control	Document Inspection	Respond to Deficiencies	Release Procured Item
Requisitioner									
Quality									
Engineering									
Safety									
Contracts									
Receiving									
Warehousing									
Property									
Project Mgmt									
Accounting									

Table 2.3 *Example of a completed row in the responsibilities table*

	Identify Procurement Need	Identify Controls	Complete Requisition Process	Receive Procured Item	Provide Storage	Conduct Receipt Control	Document Inspection
Engineering	Work with site staff to determine need for spare parts. Procurement needs identified during project design phase	Hold points may be identified in the Scope of Work Review and acceptance of submittals is required for engineering projects	Verify that material, submittal requirements are specified during requisitioning process	Construction Services (CSS) reviews for Engineering. Engineering may be present depending on project	Ensure Engineering-related items are stored according to manufacturer specifications	Conduct if required. CSS to ensure material inspection checklist is completed and item matches the approved submittal	Engineer to prepare and review material receipt inspection checklist to verify form has been properly completed

Table 2.4 *Format used for responsibility and process clarifications*

Here's What You Said	Here's the Additional Clarification the Team Requires	Here Is the Team Answer
The requisition includes • Statement of Work • Identification of permits • QA holds • Required acceptance testing	Is there guidance on what constitutes an acceptable Statement of Work?	• Template is available on intranet • Detailed process established in Engineering Manual
	What method is used to route requisitions to ensure all requirements are captured?	Required requisitioners detailed in the site responsibilities and accountabilities matrix
	How is it determined whether stipulated hold points and acceptance criteria are warranted?	Project management in conjunction with agency requesting testing or hold points reviews and makes final determination
Procurement planning identifies • Replacement parts • Item identified in design activities • Long lead-time items	How is preplanning done, by whom, and how documented?	Multiple means are used to identify procurements • Integrated work control process: project control • Items associated with leases: facilities mgmt • Project schedules: program mgmt • Validation of funding: project mgmt • Equipment inventories, audits, and assessments: safety and health
Prior to procurement, it is confirmed that items being procured are not already available in storage or excess	Who does the confirmation, how does it need to be documented (e.g., identified on the standard requisition form?)	• Different paths whether acquisition is by purchase card or standard requisition form • There is no warehouse holding spare parts • Property mgmt controls excesses • Notices issued prior to excessing equipment • Excess may also be available through GSA (Government Services Administration)

Developing Consensus

Although the team has now captured what they know about the process, who is responsible, and how it works, that does not automatically guarantee that they have agreed upon the path forward or have captured the opportunities for improvement on the final version of the responsibilities table—improvements within the receipt control process or, by extension, opportunities those changes might engender across the company.

Coming to agreement on improvements and opportunities is a separate step. As we had noted in Chapter 1, at the juncture when decisions appear to be evident, we employ Toulmin's representation of argument. The goal is to better understand, test, and ensure informed agreement that the assumptions underpinning the team members' conclusions represent the quality of sound reasoning upon which the team can proceed with confidence to finalizing a new approach to receipt control.

In advance of providing this depiction of the receipt control process, let's back out to allow a broader picture of how the receipt control process fits in the larger company context. Assume that the company has several locations, all of which procure and receive equipment and materials. These locations have different specializations and operations; operate essentially independent of one another (the prime reason senior management has requested the review); have some, but not all, procured items in common; differ in the level of training they have received regarding receipt control; and differ in that not all locations have staffing and facilities for receiving materials, storing it, and staging items for receipt inspections.

Of the five company locations, Location 1 has had the fewest number of customer complaints for five years running—a factor that has contributed to the team's conclusion that the path forward is best served by replicating the approaches used at Location 1 at all five company locations. The team is also of this opinion owing to the fact that the procedure in place, the one being evaluated, was drafted by personnel at Location 1.

Given this preliminary conclusion about modeling all sites after Location 1, among the primary questions still to be answered by the team are: Is using Location 1 as the model the best decision, and will the company and the five locations be best served by directing all locations to change their procedures consistent with the procedure used at Location 1?

Shifting the narrative momentarily from protracted team discussion to a simple representation of the team's assertions and conclusion, as we had mentioned previously, we find Toulmin's model for depicting argument is most effective at junctures such as these when the team is of the opinion that they have reached a final position. Being able to visualize the argument for using Location 1 as the standard for receipt control allows the team to fully appreciate the underlying reasoning of their decision and to gauge quickly the efficacy and appropriateness of their assessment.

In this instance, the depiction makes it readily apparent that there are areas requiring further analysis. In particular, the visualization makes evident that the "warrant" and the "grounds" need further examination (Figure 2.2).

The immediate question regarding the warrant is whether the team has validated the assumption that the types and volumes of procurements requiring receipt inspections will remain stable for the foreseeable future. In this instance, so as not to overly complicate our example, let's accept that the team has done its due diligence on this topic; it has confirmed through an evaluation of long-term procurement planning that the company anticipates no significant changes in the types and volumes of materials and equipment to be ordered over the next few years.

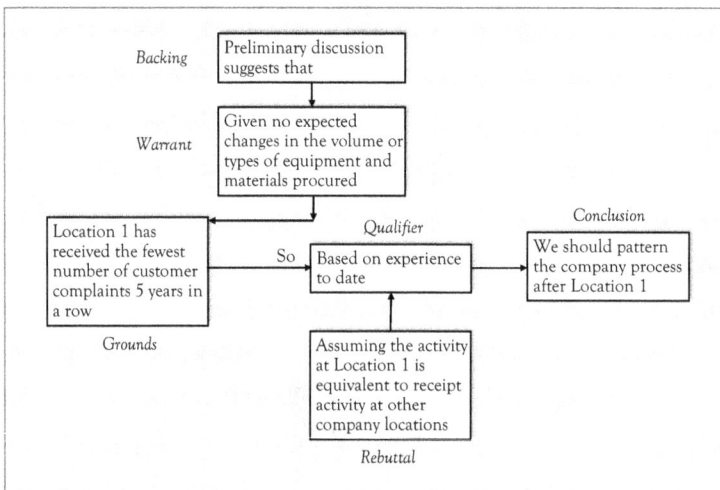

Figure 2.2 Depiction of the logic of the team's initial conclusion

With the warrant validated, the focus of the expanded examination next needs to address the principal basis underpinning the team's assertion: The team has accepted the fact that the location experiencing the fewest complaints, by definition, must be the best performing location and, therefore, is best suited to serve as the model for the other four company locations.

Yet, having raised the visibility of this assumption, in order to substantiate the grounds and conclusion of the argument, the team must convince themselves of two underlying assumptions: (1) Having the fewest complaints is a direct consequence of the superior performance in all segments of activity identified in the responsibilities table; and (2) using the number of complaints as a metric is a sound basis on which to predicate the decision to have other locations replicate the practices in place at Location 1.

Answering the first question entails a review of two related areas of analysis: Why did Location 1 not get as many complaints as the other locations and what specifically were the themes (and causes) of the complaints experienced at other sites?

Let's assume that, to answer these questions, the team obtains copies of all the complaints for all locations over the past year. What they find is a pattern: Complaints tend to flag issues of timeliness of deliveries, the frequency of changes in cost from one order to the next, and slow processing and release of the item once received at the company site. In particular, when examined in more depth, the complaints are almost all associated with locations that have one or more of four defining characteristics not part of the design at Location 1: They have the fewest resources for receiving and inspecting shipments; regularly procure sensitive materials or hazardous materials that require special handling practices; routinely engage in maintaining specially designed, one-of-a-kind equipment requiring acquisition of long lead time items; and do not have access to the company's automated procurement system, rather relying on a number of tasks that must be done and recorded manually.

Based on this additional information, the team now has its answers to both of its questions: (1) They definitely require more information before a model can be selected, and, perhaps, (2) the number of complaints may not be the most appropriate criterion on which to make their final judgment about using Location 1 as a model for all five locations.

Securing Commitment

Securing commitment is a condition achieved by having collected and sifted through a sufficient range and depth of material so as to provide a high level of confidence in the assertions and conclusions being reached. In this regard, as we had mentioned earlier in the chapter, to establish the foundation for advancing enrichment beyond the dimensions of a single procedure, attention paid to enhancing the process must be accompanied by similar depth of study of the impacts and implications of such process factors as process variables, constraints, and interfaces.

Variables: As we just noted, the review of complaints made evident to the team that there was a great deal of difference among the locations as regards administration of the receipt control process. Following up on that topic, additional research by the team highlighted the fact that no two locations had the same scope of work or approach to conducting receipt control.

Tasks: Most significant of these findings is the fact that Location 1 had none of the four conditions that the team had identified as most likely to result in complaints owing to longer lead times, order discrepancies, and cost deviations (Table 2.5).

Although in their original conclusion the team had allowed for the fact that there were differences in the way receipt control was being conducted at each of the sites, it was not until the additional research was conducted and appropriately displayed that the magnitude and areas of difference were fully delineated. Rather than dealing with an issue of five variations (i.e., the five sites), defining a path forward requires that each of the areas of difference (each row on Table 2.5) be addressed in the team's reformulation of the process. Only with that fully informed approach can a recommendation be posited that considers the full breadth of implications (the magnitude and practical challenges) at each of the locations.

Given the number of variations in play, the team challenge is to recognize that any number of alternative solutions may exist. The simplest

Table 2.5 Comparison of location capabilities

	Location 1	Location 2	Location 3	Location 4	Location 5
Dedicated property management personnel on site	Y	Y	Y	N	N
Access to company property management system	Y	Y	N	N	N
Automated procurement process	Y	N	N	N	N
Technical staff (e.g., engineering) on site	Y	Y	Y	N	Y
Orders and receives sensitive material	N	N	Y	N	Y
Warehouse capability on site	Y	N	N	Y	N
Deliveries to field as well as office	N	N	N	Y	Y
Personnel trained in receipt control	Y	Y	Y	N	Y
Location receives hazardous materials	N	N	N	Y	N
Location relies on corporate capability (e.g., accounts payable)	N	N	N	N	Y
Majority of procurements are for standard off-the-shelf items	Y	Y	N	Y	N

would be, as the team initially proposed, to choose one location as the model and then require that all locations institute that same process.

Looking back at the early stages of scientific management, as we had previously noted, that is primarily the way standardization had historically been imposed. Originators of scientific management like Frederick Taylor monitored how different workers performed a specific task and then isolated and eliminated steps they thought extraneous or redundant. The remaining steps became the operating standard for all employees.

Yet, while a company will generally strive to standardize operations so as to have the highest confidence in the efficiency, safety, and compliance of a process, simply overlaying one approach on top of all functions or all corporate locations without careful analysis of the implications is potentially a recipe for failure. For instance, using Table 2.5 as a guide, had the original team recommendation to use Location 1 as a model been mandated, all sites would have been detrimentally affected—some saddled with capabilities and resources they had no use for, and others deprived of ability to respond to the full suite of commodities and equipment being received. In all instances, the company would incur unwarranted and indefensible expenditures, not to mention potentially introducing issues of worker satisfaction.

Now, in comparison, equipped with knowledge of the variations that must be accommodated in any solution, the team needs to further its knowledge and appreciation of the challenge by considering two additional factors: constraints and interfaces.

Constraints: While variations pertain to the numerous ways the process or components of the process are being performed, constraints refer to expectations, requirements, and commitments that are imposed on the system. They are factors that must become part of the process design. In some cases, constraints might be specific steps that need to be called out (for instance, if a regulation stipulates that a certain hazardous chemical must be labeled and stored according to a precise set of specifications); in other instances, the constraints may be generalized limitations or ranges (for instance, the airport weight limitations that had to be accommodated in Delta Airlines' fleet assignment challenge as discussed in the Introduction).

The constraints on any process may be a combination of two categories: (1) externally imposed constraints, constraints established by organizations, agencies, regulators, and, even, stakeholders that are outside the company's authority and must be implemented; and (2) company-mandated constraints, limitations, and operational boundaries enacted by the company.

The externally imposed boundaries may be easy to identify, but often represent the most complicated to implement. This difficulty arises from the fact that laws and regulations are not only a mixture of specific requirements and generalized expectations, but also generally intended to be applied across whole industries—meaning that only limited segments of a law or regulation are likely to be applicable to any particular company or corporation.

Take for example the potential variations possible for implementing a single component of the Code of Federal Regulation requirements for labeling hazardous materials—an externally imposed constraint that may affect the receipt control operations at Location 4:

> *Contrast with background.* Each label must be printed on or affixed to a background color contrasting to the color specification of the label as required by §172.407(d)(1), or must have a dotted or solid line outer border, to enhance the visibility of the label. However, the dotted or solid line outer border may also be used for backgrounds of contrasting color. CFR Title 49, Part 172 (172.406(d))

Further, to ensure the continued integrity of any procedure, the ability to ensure that revisions of the procedure don't inadvertently result in noncompliances with externally imposed constraints, often a company must create some form of record or matrix to demonstrate how and by which procedures program compliance is established.

As was the case on a project we supported in the United Kingdom, the company was required to make

> a commitment to retain sufficient safety related knowledge, expertise, and experience to understand the hazards associated with its operations and how to control them. One critical element of providing this continued assurance is . . . a system that demonstrates that pertinent obligations are known, have been factored into the modes of doing business, and that there is a means of maintaining current with new and amended obligations.[6]

The means by which this obligation was validated, and a format we have applied in several contracts, was a very detailed compliance matrix (Figure 2.3).

Section I. Site Wide Compliance Detail

Applicable sections to be completed by Process Owner
(in conjunction with Process Manager)

Element:								
	A. Adequate Documentation Currently Exists			**B. New/Revised Documentation Required**			**C. No Documentation Required**	**D. Facility-Specific Documentation Required**	**E. Records Generated**
Specific Obligation Completed by Management Systems Compliance Manager	Document Citation	Specific Implementation Detail	Notes/ Clarifications	Citation–and Specific Need	Issue Schedule	Respon-sibility	Specific Explanation	Yes No	

Compliance Matrix

Section II. Facility Compliance Detail

☐ Effluent Plants   ☐ Encapsulation Plants   ☐ High-Level Waste Plants   ☐ Magnox

☐ Thorp   ☐ Windscale   ☐ MOX   ☐ Waste Plants

To Be Completed by Operating Facility Management

Element:						
	A. Adequate Documentation Currently Exists			**B. New/revised Documentation Required**		**C. Records Generated**
Completed by Management Systems Compliance Manager	Document Citation	Specific Implementation Detail	Notes/ Clarifications	Citation and Specific Need	Issue Schedule	Responsible Individual
Specific Obligation	Site-level Implementing Document (from Sec I)					

Figure 2.3 Example of a matrix documenting compliance with constraints

In contrast to externally imposed constraints, internally mandated constraints derive from two directions: vertically down through a succession of company documents and horizontally as requirements established by one segment of the company upon another.

Depending on the company size and complexity of operations, companies may employ a hierarchy of documents. Descending from the externally imposed requirements, this hierarchy cascades downward beginning with policies that articulate management's expectations and finally arriving at the process or task level. As shown in Figure 2.4, the document types are designed to fulfill different purposes and are generally directed at different communities within the company.

At the same time that influences and constraints may be flowing down to the process under evaluation, other company programs or outside agencies may also set constraints on the process. As was reflected in Table 2.2, many organizations can contribute to defining how a process is administered. In addition, a range of circumstances associated with these contributing organizations may affect the process. For example, there may be certain materials required by the process that become back ordered resulting in process shutdowns, or any of the 10 business risks cited in Chapter 1 may adversely affect the process depending on how dependent the process is on other company programs and outside forces.

In the case of receipt control, for instance, program limitations and requirements are set by a handful of other company programs:

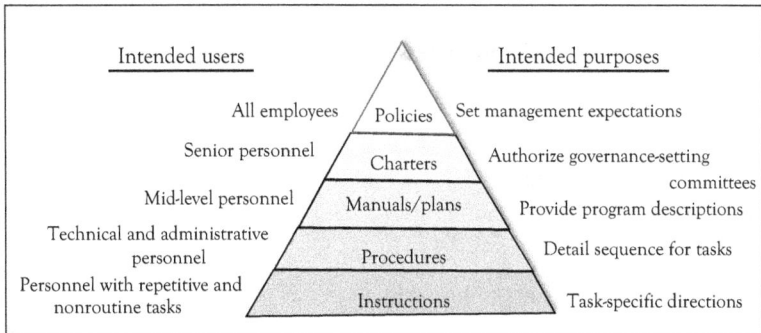

Figure 2.4 Example of company document hierarchy

- Construction: identifies the equipment and materials to be received consistent with requirements of project as-built documentation and performs the associated receipt inspections
- Engineering: defines equipment and material specifications forming the basis for procurement and receipt activities
- Environmental management: identifies regulatory and industry standards and requirements to be confirmed upon receipt
- Facility management: provides for receiving, storing, handling, and disposition of received materials and equipment
- Property management: defines the processes for labeling of and accountability for received material and equipment
- Procurement: establishes the acquisition process, detailing requirements for planning, receipt, acceptance, and release of materials and equipment
- Quality assurance: sets receipt criteria and is the primary agency responsible for conducting receipt inspections and disposition of deficient receipts
- Safety and health: establishes specifications and receipt criteria for equipment and materials associated with safety systems, pressurized systems, and personal protection

Interfaces: Corporate programs and processes rarely operate in isolation. The points of intersections among processes constitute the interfaces that need to be examined if a comprehensive assessment is to be completed. Related to constraints, these interfaces define the inputs and outputs, the points at which processes are interdependent. However, unlike constraints, interfaces do not necessarily establish limitations or boundaries on one another, but, rather, constitute handoffs that initiate segments of the process or are deliverables provided to another process.

If we reconsider some of the programs that potentially may be the source of constraints on the receipt control process, we might anticipate commonly experienced effects resulting when one process undergoes change: Forms used to communicate between programs may need to be redesigned, for example, property management records or documentation of inspections; communication channels may be simplified or augmented, as in the automation of shared information between the warehouse and quality assurance; or responsibilities in one or more programs may be reassigned, combined, or eliminated, as in the potential need to transfer and reassign personnel from one company location to another.

As is the case with constraints, a change in inputs and outputs can have a cascading effect beyond the initially affected processes. A single change in inputs or outputs may, in turn, trigger changes in the interfaces further downstream (Figure 2.5).

For our purposes of discussion, recognizing the interfaces immediate to the receipt control process is sufficient. However, it should be recognized that when the goal is to promote a broad-based set of enrichments, the full complement of cascading interfaces is the means by which to trace the path across the breadth of the company.

A Re-evaluation

Having now considered the full range of variations, constrains, and interfaces, the team can confidently reconsider their conclusions. The analysis of variations has made evident that simply using complaints as a measure of success is inappropriate since the circumstances and challenges for Location 1 are different from (and seemingly less demanding) than challenges faced by other locations. Analysis of constraints makes clear that certain allowances or accommodations are going to be necessary if all constraints and boundaries are going to be effectively addressed with a practical and implementable solution. Further, analysis of the immediate interfaces of the process indicates adjustments within the receipt control process are likely to have direct and immediate consequences on the design of the activities and program that are interconnected with it—design changes that when taken in total represent the landscape of broad-based corporate enrichment.

With this much clearer evidence-based perspective regarding the dimensions of the task at hand and the field beyond, the team can now with greater confidence recast the elements of the argument in order to take another look, knowledgeable that the original formulation—patterning all locations after the process employed at Location 1—is no longer a reasonable solution and aware that the associated "grounds" and

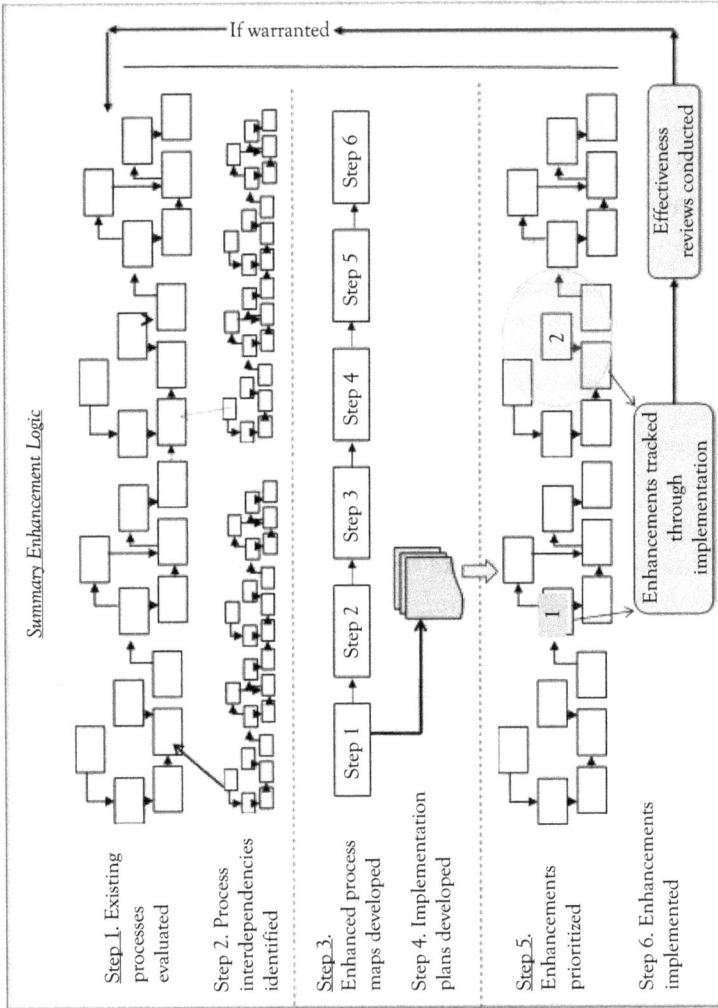

Figure 2.5 The interrelationship of interfaces

"qualifier" in their representation of that conclusion have been appropriately adjusted.

Discussion of the variations that exist and the different constraints imposed on various locations provides the foundation the team needed to identify and evaluate options. Although slight permutations exist, the information analyzed provides the reasoning for a determination regarding which of the three principal options available to them is the most reasoned:

Option 1: As originally proposed, select one location and make the others conform to it. However, further consideration and analysis has demonstrated that the associated expense would be unreasonable and would, rather than creating five locations that function efficiently, result in a misalignment between the local operations and its capabilities. Location 1, as example, would have specially designed capability to manage hazardous materials that it is never going to receive.

Option 2: Create a single location designed to handle all manner and volume of company procurements for all five locations. Although some efficiencies might accrue, the implementation costs—designing and building facilities and warehouses; equipping and staffing a new transportation fleet—compounded by possible adverse impacts on each location's ability to meet schedule and commitments make this an undesirable option.

Option 3: Institute a process that has three distinct components: (a) It establishes a set of attributes and mandatory requirements with which every location must comply; (b) it allows each location to tailor its receipt control practices (within the confines of the requirements) to accommodate the site's unique needs; and (c) it establishes the means and authorities to monitor and audit site compliance.

No longer predicated on the basis of which site has the fewest complaints, Option 3 is directly responsive to the implicit set of team-defined criteria. Imbedded in this solution are the criteria that establish an approach that:

- Introduces a reasoned approach to consistency
- Accommodates the needed degree of variation among the locations

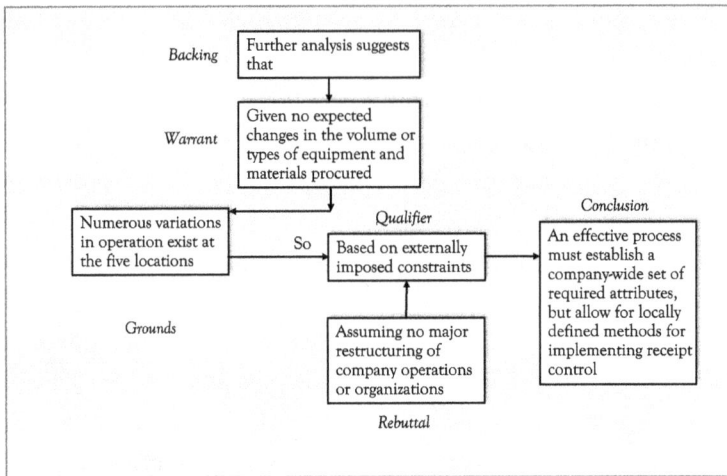

Figure 2.6 The team's restatement of the argument

- Precludes unwarranted costs
- Avoids jeopardizing schedules
- Implements a balance between local and corporate authority
- Assures compliance to internally and externally imposed constraints
- Promotes corporate harmony

As was done with the depiction of the team's initial conclusion, the argument is again depicted using Toulmin's model. The difference now is that rather than being the source for raising questions and for identifying areas needing further investigation and analysis, this time the model depicts the basis of an informed consensus (Figure 2.6).

Creating a Community of Purpose

Having arrived at a consensus, the team can now begin to translate their conclusions into recommendations. In keeping with the insights provided by the Toulmin model, and with consideration of the hierarchy of company document types, the team can develop a clear path forward.

At the immediate level of implementation is the introduction of the new receipt control process. As one means of laying out this new structure, it will be necessary to explain to all the impacted company organizations how the new process was derived. A particularly effective means of accomplishing this task is to provide a segment-by-segment explanation of what is expected and how it is to be delivered.

Using a slightly abbreviated list of expectations, Table 2.5 uses the segments originally identified by the team (Table 2.2). The first column summarizes the associated attributes of an effective receipt control. As was just indicated in the representation of the team's conclusion (Figure 2.6), "an effective process must establish a company-wide set of required attributes but allows for locally defined methods for implementing receipt control."

Stated in terms of a company document hierarchy, at the top of the pyramid, there are attributes derived from the constraints applicable to the process. These attributes are then translated into a company policy—the document codifying management's expectations for all employees. The third column indicates how those expectations are proceduralized (i.e., implemented at each location).

In this particular case, the change in policy likely will result in five procedures—one for each of the company locations. Those procedures will be a blend (as shown in the farthest left column of Table 2.6) of accepting the flow down of particular elements of the company policy, complemented by specific, individualized practices tailored to the needs and capabilities of each location.

Once the set of new procedures has been drafted, the team has fulfilled its first initiative—to revise the process flow. However, as we have asserted, a comprehensive approach to company enrichment sees process changes as only one of the categories of opportunity. The team next needs to move to another one of the five points of enrichment identified previously: automating processes, enhancing training, redefining protocols and governance, and re-evaluating strategies.

Conclusion

Returning to the glider built in the attic of Colditz Castle, the timing that had precluded the launching of the glider left military history with two enduring questions: (1) Would the glider actually have flown, and, if so,

Table 2.6 Implementing the team's recommendations

Process Segment	Attribute	Elements of the Company Policy	Elements of the Location-Specific Procedures
Identify procurement need	• Pre-procurement planning is required • Procurement needs are validated • Annual independent audits are conducted confirming compliance with regulations	• Long-term procurement needs must be annually updated • Major project-related purchases must be identified on project schedules • Requestors must validate the item is not available in storage or through excess	• A specific process is set up to document long-term procurement planning • The procedure explains how local personnel are to be certified by the Procurement Department to act as authorized buyers
Identify controls	• Requisitions (other than for off-the-shelf commodities) receive appropriate reviews • Requisitions identify all required receipt actions • Funds availability is validated prior to requisition approval	A company-controlled matrix identifies required reviews for • Field services equipment • Hazardous materials • Safety equipment • Furniture • Computing equipment	• The standard requisition form in the company Procurement Manual is used • Required receipt actions are added to the company list; designated personnel are identified
Complete requisition process	• Only authorized personnel can commit company funds • Only procurement personnel can communicate formally with vendors	Only the procurement organization and buyers certified by them can place orders and negotiate with vendors	• The procedure details how local personnel are certified to act as agents of the Procurement Department

Receive procured item	• All accountable property must be entered in the company property management system • All receipts must be validated against the requisition • Items are handled as designated	Personnel are directed to follow company manuals: • Procurement • Property Management • Quality Assurance	• The references in the company policy are reproduced in the local procedure
Provide storage	• Appropriate storage for procurements is provided	• Storage must be provided that protects against loss, theft, destruction, or deterioration	• Controls are established consistent with local needs, e.g., separate, approved storage is provided for hazardous materials
Conduct receipt control	• All designated receipt control actions must be completed by qualified personnel	• The company-controlled matrix lists the controls and qualified organizations	• The local matrix identifies all additional qualified personnel
Document inspection	• All receipt actions are to be documented	• Records of receipt actions must be filed with property management, including notation of dates, results, and additional actions	• A local inspection form consistent with QA and property requirements is developed
Respond to deficiencies	• All deficiencies in procurements can only be resolved by authorized personnel	• All deficiencies must be resolved by the procurement organization	• The local-certified personnel handle communications and coordination with vendors
Release procured item	• Release of the item must be documented	• A standard form available in the Property Manual is to be used for all personal and sensitive property	• The designated form is used at all locations

(2) would it have safely carried its crew (two British officers) the 300 to 500 yards to the castle's boundary or beyond?

The answers to these questions were provided some 66 years after the original glider was scheduled to have flown. In 2011, the owner of South East Aircraft Services (a company specializing in glider maintenance, modifications, and repairs) was contracted by a British film company to build a replica of the Colditz glider.

Built according to the prisoners' design and specifications; con-structed, to the degree reasonable, of materials similar to those available to the prisoners; and similarly propelled using the weight of a concrete-filled bathtub, the manned glider—as was the plan for its predecessor—was to be launched from the roof of Colditz Castle.

A few months later, the glider team brought their replica to Colditz Castle, positioned it on the roof, secured the bathtub, and launched the glider. Just as the prisoners had planned in 1945, the glider took off and landed safely in the designated target area.

> Dipping off the end of the runway, the glider began descending rapidly . . . Then I heard the crack of the impact of the concrete-filled bathtub as it ploughed into the cushioning pile of timber and sandbags . . . The glider seemed to be flying fine, and was carrying a reasonable amount of speed. . . . [H]aving cleared the trees, . . . it was within the field boundary. The wing contacted the ground . . . and the whole thing stopped abruptly . . . [T]he glider . . . had landed. . . . We had done it.[7]

Continuing the metaphor, we might ask, so where have we landed? As we have been explaining in these first two chapters, unlike the two extreme conditions—the multifaceted, overly complex challenge of the Delta Airlines fleet assignment or the overwhelmingly handicapped circumstances of building and launching a glider in a prisoner-of-war camp—analyzing and optimizing the vast majority of company processes demand considerably less computational capability, are bounded by sig-nificantly fewer inviolable externally imposed constraints, and have fewer significant adverse consequences of failure.

Rather, the challenges we likely face in optimizing administrative, technical, or safety practices and in so doing securing a pathway to pursuing broader company enrichment begin with five essential elements:

- Selecting an appropriate team
- Instilling that team with a culture of knowledge, commitment, and reasonableness
- Complementing that culture with a set of behaviors that promote cooperation, confidence, and a bias for action
- Pursuing a thorough appreciation of the process including its variations, constraints, and interfaces
- Promoting a systematic assessment by employing a disciplined and readily implementable analytical methodology designed to deliver sound and appropriate conclusions and recommendations

Having secured these elements, the team is now ready and prepared to start considering branching out from the process initially addressed to delving into the broader range of corporate optimization opportunities that now begin to unfold, beginning with considering automating the process it has just designed.

CHAPTER 3

Tailoring Technology

*The Pacific Railroad will [soon] realize its advantages. . . . The day is
not far distant when three tracks will . . . accommodate the commerce
which will seek transit across this continent. Freights will then move . . .
at rates of speed that will answer the demand of cheapness and time.*

—Leland Stanford
Promontory Summit, Utah
May 10, 1869[1]

Leland Stanford, eighth governor of California and later U.S. Senator
from that state, was also president of both the Central Pacific and the
Southern Pacific Railroads. In that last capacity, on May 10, 1869, at
Promontory Summit, Utah, he drove the golden spike joining the existing eastern railroad network with the Union Pacific and Central Pacific
Railroads, creating the nation's first intercontinental railway. Yet his leg-
acy is most often associated with having given his name to and founding
grant for Stanford University, a school whose purpose (as he stipulated) is
committed to providing the "studies and exercises directed to the cultiva-
tion and enlargement of the mind."[2]

A man of the Senator's expansive perspective, business acumen, progressive orientation, and entrepreneurial spirit would surely have been a
shrewd investor when it came to recognizing and assessing technological
advances trumpeted as being on the cusp of reinventing society. Then,
again, maybe not.

In 1882, in the first of his two patents (Patent U.S. 260,657), William
Calver described his "Method of and Means for Utilizing the Rays of the
Sun," an invention designed for "reflecting, directing, and concentrating
the rays of the sun and utilizing the same for heating or other purposes
and as a source of power." Multiple reflectors mounted in an array on an
adjustable platform would each direct a beam of concentrated sunlight at

a target. However, unlike a single concentrated beam as occurs with the use of a magnifying glass, the beams would be projected in parallel, each adding its power and intensity to the next. The cumulative power—"the excessive heat" generated—Calver asserted in the patent, produced energy sufficient to melt "wrought-iron . . . in the open air and shade."[3]

A few years later in a patent initially filed in 1895 and awarded in 1898 (Patent U.S. 603,317), Calver offered "certain new and useful" design enhancements to this "Solar Apparatus": "automatic control of the various necessary movements of parts of the apparatus, their adjustment, and the simplification of the structure."

However, more significant in advancing the invention's attractiveness was its distinctly defined commercial application. Not only did the design adjustments allow the machine's use throughout the "different seasons of the year," it had, according to the patent, been

> adapted for the production of steam, and in this regard, . . . possess[ed] novel and advantageous features, while at the same time the invention . . . [remained] capable of application for various and any other purposes for which the solar rays may be employed.[4]

The power of the sun unleashed by Archimedes in his war against Marcellus and the Romans had, supposedly, finally been harnessed some 20 centuries later. No longer an instrument limited to a single application in war, the concentrating of the sun's rays was being heralded as the potential source of all energy needed to power homes and industry.

Having been introduced by its inventor to this "helio-motor," a supposed sun-driven source of infinite energy, Senator Stanford proclaimed that Calver's solar apparatus "will do more for humanity than all we have at present. The steam engine made a great revolution, and this will make another, and a greater."[5]

With endorsements of that caliber, it was not long before the press began hawking this invention as destined to change the world. Full-page newspaper articles across the country explored the grandiose possibilities: "Has He Harnessed the Sun's Rays" (*St. Louis Republic*) (Figure 3.1) [6]; "Are Steam and Electricity Doomed to Fall Before Concentrated Sunpower?" (*San Francisco Call*).[7] Yet even these localized endorsements did not rival

Figure 3.1 Calver and his invention—St. Louis Republic

the spectacular prospects projected in an article in *Pearson's Magazine*, a popular journal of literature, politics, and art.

Not only did the journal article, "Tapping the Sun's Rays," echo Calver's claim that the power of the invention could be used to bring water at an "insignificant cost" to semi-arid ranges like the American southwest, it went on to suggest the helio-motor presaged a total redefinition of the American industrial landscape:

> with the sun motor in commercial use, it will be no longer necessary to denude the forests or delve into the bowels of the earth before we can heat our houses or make the steam required in our factories, railroads, and ships.[8]

Unfortunately for the investors who flocked to get in on this popularized, world-changing phenomenon, lacking the superconductive materials needed to translate such power into practical large-scale usage (a capability still eluding scientists today), Calver's helio-motor could do little more to advance commerce and industry than did the ray Archimedes had invented 20 centuries earlier. The invention consequently faded quickly from public view along with the investors' money.

As the episode with Dr. Calver and Leland Stanford suggests, technology can be enticing—whether looking for a means to redefine a culture, an economy, or a single process. As one of the common themes of our approach again proves, for every investment—financial or otherwise—there needs to be a reasoned approach.

But before we get to that discussion of applying a reasoned approach to the selection and implementation of automation or technology, we need to build the bridge from process improvement, as just accomplished by our team, to the introduction of a broadened target of optimization.

Broadening the enhancement opportunity: Having answered the question of how to handle the challenge of a multiple location process for receipt control, the team must determine how the intended improvements are to be implemented—how to make the performance of the proposed process reliable, consistent, and predictable. A starting point for this set of determinations is to evaluate if the process or select process segments are good candidates to automate or if technology might supplant manual sequences.

To assist in such considerations, the agreed to process flow must be laid out. Commonly, processes (whether technical or administrative) are articulated in one of three narrative procedure formats: (1) standard paragraph format; (2) individual steps separated by paragraph returns; or in (3) "swim lanes," a matrix in which columns delineate contributing organizations and rows list individual process steps, each positioned in the column corresponding to the responsible individual or organization.

Interspersed within the body of the procedure are notes of explanation; warnings and cautions alerting the user to hazards or risks associated with specific process steps; and references to interrelated practices that may inform the particular action. Also, as would be expected given our earlier discussion regarding the means by which the team arrived at the proposed process, embedded in the procedure are acknowledgments of variations, constraints, and interfaces.

Given this range of elements that may compose the procedure, it is not hard to appreciate that providing teams with multipage text documents is not going to be very conducive to encouraging ready recognition of further opportunities for enhancement. Rather, as was the case when we used the Toulmin model to assess the team's bases and conclusions, visualization is the key.

Providing a consolidated depiction of the process is the best means to allow the team to grasp the bigger (complete) picture. Without that broader perspective, thinking is subject to being relegated to the type of narrowing of vision that contributed to the team's original (incorrect—and potentially unworkable) solution on how to improve the company's receipt control process.

To provide the team with a consolidated vision, we use a process flowsheet. Incorporating the full range of process elements (as just described), the format is—for all intents and purposes—the expanded logic employed by Toulmin. However, rather than highlighting a summary level of factors underpinning the argument, the flowchart lays out the detailed implementation consequent to concluding the argument. As in the Toulmin model, a simple structure is employed (Figure 3.2).

Using this notation scheme, an entire process (such as the team's reformulation of the receipt control process) can be displayed on one or a few pages. The chart can also be enlarged, mounted, and remain a visual aide throughout the course of the team discussions (Figure 3.3).

Type of Step	How Illustrated	Application
Action		Denotes a single task to be completed
Decision		One or more options are possible, often consequent to a constraint
Move elsewhere in the procedure		Allows for efficiently incorporating variations and identifying key process interfaces
Clarification		Adds explanations/context to process steps—often explaining constraints and interfaces
Warning		Identifies a risk or hazard associated with the steps or sequence immediately following the symbol
End of process sequence		Denotes the sequence or the process is complete

Figure 3.2 Basic elements of the process flowsheet

FLOWCHART A

Procurement need identified

R1
Long-lead time pre procurement planning conducted

R2
Contracts prequalifies long-lead time items and major equipment vendors

G1
Items available in storage or excess (GSA surplus link)?
Yes / No

NOTE: Long-lead time items identified
- replacement parts
- during design activities and development of project schedules
- during Integrated Work Control Process
- as needed in leased buildings
- during life cycle budget planning

P1
P-card purchase?
No / Yes

Go to Flowchart C

Go to Step R6

G2
Requester contacts a procurement professional authorized to request GSA surplus items

R3
Initiate requisition (Form 90)

R4
Confirm funding availability and schedule requirements with Program Management

R5
Draft requisition:
- Scope of work
- Technical Requirements
- Documentation
- Acceptance of items and services
- Graded flow down of requirements

G3
Item is requested from storage and GSA and provided to requester

R6
Conduct required reviews and establish receipt, inspection, holds, and storage criteria:
- Field services and equipment–EC, S&H, Engineering;
- Radioactive sources and hazardous materials–S&H RadCon and EC;
- Safety equipment and PPE–S&H;
- Furniture–S&H ergonomist;
- Commodities and other receipt inspections as requested–as appropriate (e.g., QA)
- Computing equipment–IT
- As identified in PAEs, JSAs, and Construction specifications–Site Ops

R7
Complete sign-off by responsible funds manager

R8
Order placed; P6 schedule updated for major project-related procurements; requester and asset management notified

END OF PROCESS

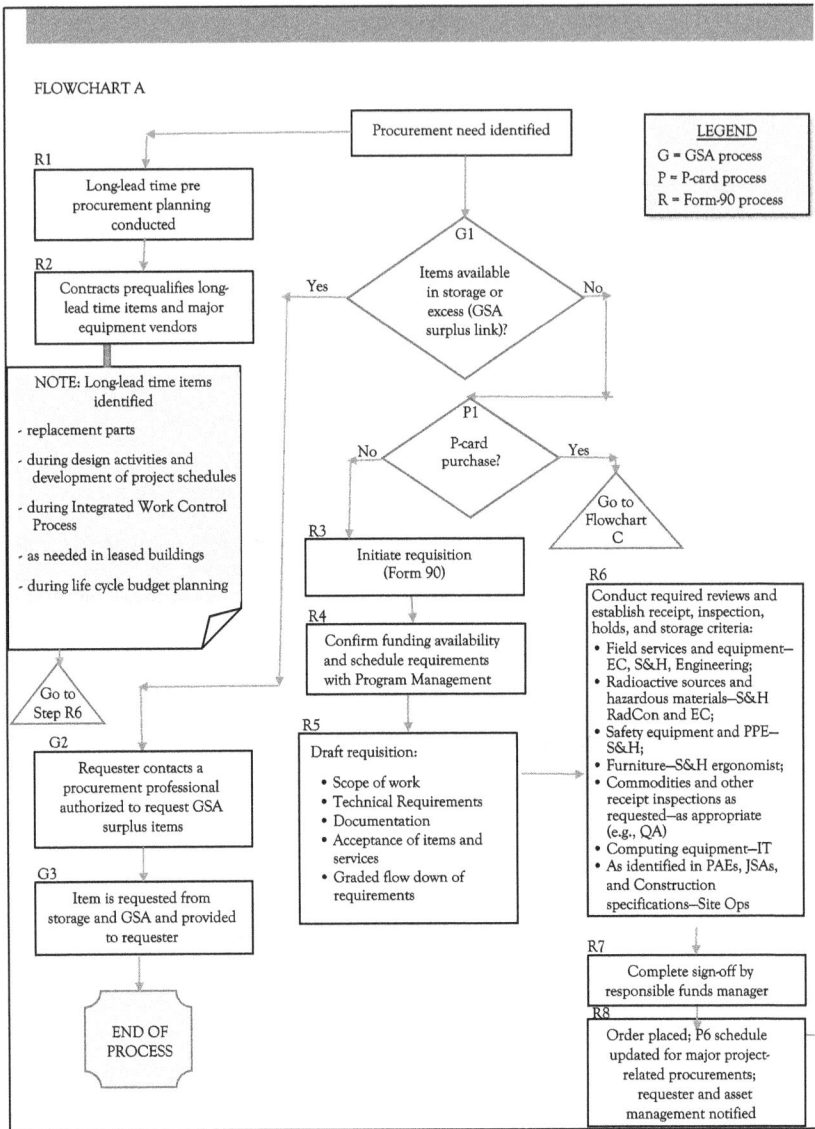

Figure 3.3 Sample team-developed procedure flowchart

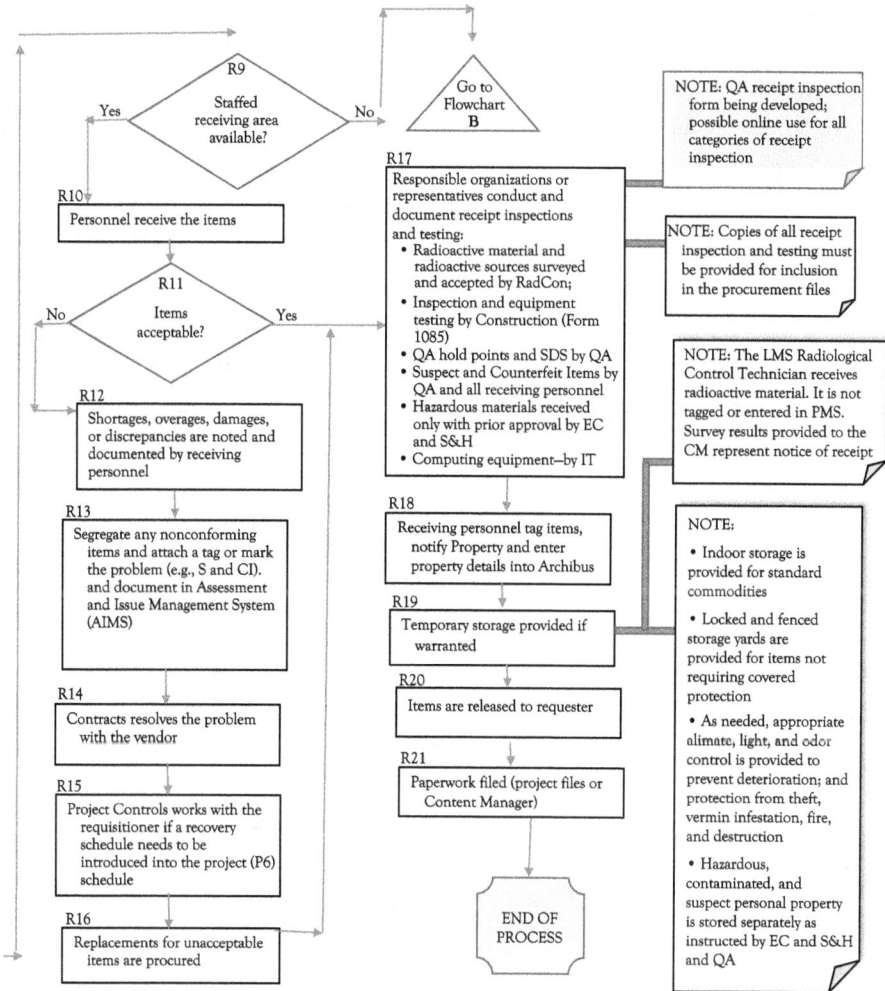

R9 Staffed receiving area available?

Yes → **R10** Personnel receive the items

No → Go to Flowchart **B**

R11 Items acceptable?

No → **R12** Shortages, overages, damages, or discrepancies are noted and documented by receiving personnel

R13 Segregate any nonconforming items and attach a tag or mark the problem (e.g., S and CI). and document in Assessment and Issue Management System (AIMS)

R14 Contracts resolves the problem with the vendor

R15 Project Controls works with the requisitioner if a recovery schedule needs to be introduced into the project (P6) schedule

R16 Replacements for unacceptable items are procured

R17 Responsible organizations or representatives conduct and document receipt inspections and testing:
- Radioactive material and radioactive sources surveyed and accepted by RadCon;
- Inspection and equipment testing by Construction (Form 1085)
- QA hold points and SDS by QA
- Suspect and Counterfeit Items by QA and all receiving personnel
- Hazardous materials received only with prior approval by EC and S&H
- Computing equipment—by IT

R18 Receiving personnel tag items, notify Property and enter property details into Archibus

R19 Temporary storage provided if warranted

R20 Items are released to requester

R21 Paperwork filed (project files or Content Manager)

END OF PROCESS

NOTE: QA receipt inspection form being developed; possible online use for all categories of receipt inspection

NOTE: Copies of all receipt inspection and testing must be provided for inclusion in the procurement files

NOTE: The LMS Radiological Control Technician receives radioactive material. It is not tagged or entered in PMS. Survey results provided to the CM represent notice of receipt

NOTE:
- Indoor storage is provided for standard commodities
- Locked and fenced storage yards are provided for items not requiring covered protection
- As needed, appropriate climate, light, and odor control is provided to prevent deterioration; and protection from theft, vermin infestation, fire, and destruction
- Hazardous, contaminated, and suspect personal property is stored separately as instructed by EC and S&H and QA

Technology Selection

With the process redefined and illustrated, it becomes a straightforward effort to start identifying technology opportunities. Sometimes the changes are merely a matter of utilizing existing software or intranets. As example, in this instance, basic software made available on the company's intranet might be programmed to link procurement actions at all five sites. Or it might be used to create links among the property, procurement, and warehouse databases to automate managing company inventories as well as receipt control. In other instances, process changes can trigger massive technological change. As example, the enhanced process may have resulted in a plan to automate warehouse operations. Irrespective of the magnitude or type of technology to be introduced, much as was the case in choosing team members, the selection process requires careful analysis.

Although not all factors will apply in every instance, and their relative importance will change with the unique circumstances in play, thoughtful technology selection entails consideration of 10 primary factors:

1. Features: Beginning by establishing a comprehensive list of requirements, determine technologies or software that are best aligned with those needs. To the degree reasonable, preference should be given to products that can be used without substantive, localized configuration. Generally, the more modifications, the more difficult it will be to maintain the technology as equipment is replaced or software upgraded.

2. Usability: Look for technology or software that is easy to understand and operate. Assuming only the engineers or the information technology (IT) staff need to be comfortable with the product will lead to several issues: Personnel including those individuals intended to work with the technology may become frustrated or experience problems that, in turn, require external support to fulfill responsibilities—essentially requiring the IT support, for example, to act as the default operators, tutors, maintenance team, and help desk.

3. Security: Make certain the product meets whatever security requirements that may apply, for example, appropriate restrictions on access,

protection of personnel information, isolation of company-sensitive information.

4. Flexibility: Recognizing that company practices and strategies are routinely evolving, considerations should include the degree and complexity of adapting the technology—how it operates, along with this level of difficulty likely to be experienced if adjustments are needed to accommodate changes in constraints, inputs, outputs, or interfaces.

5. Interoperability: Considering the interfaces also requires attention to how the technology or software interfaces with other technologies that it supports or is supported by. Mismatches—as in software products that can't "talk" to each other—can result in significant rework, reconfiguration, and additive costs. Also, ease of integration, like the ease of use, translates into quickly realizing the technology benefits rather than being engaged in protracted implementation and testing cycles.

6. Innovation: A consideration related to flexibility is the degree to which the technology meets future needs. On one side of the equation is responsiveness to both anticipated and unanticipated adjustments in company strategies—major redefinitions in course beyond the types of localized adjustments considered in the technology's flexibility. On the other side of the equation are matters relative to the frequency with which the supplier issues upgrades, revisions, and patches—each of which will need local support and, potentially, process or policy adjustments.

7. Costs: Several categories of costs may be involved in the selection of technology or software: (a) setup costs associated with whatever efforts are needed in the design, configuration, and rollout of the product; (b) licensing costs, which may take any of several forms, for example, annual fees, seat charges per user; and (c) maintenance and operating costs, the costs for maintaining the technology, including corrective and preventive maintenance costs, as well as costs for adaptations and upgrades.

8. Public receptivity: Although limited in its concern, certain technologies may not be well received by your customer or your workforce, especially if the firm or its products have a reputation or public

image associated with ethical lapses or questionable reliability, or are deemed otherwise inappropriate (as could be the case, for instance, with unpopular military technologies).

9. Legal and regulatory compliance: Depending on the types of technology or software, there may be statutory or regulatory requirements. For example, if your company was relying on contracted technology to meet railway transportation safety criteria, you would want to make certain who held the liability in the event of a safety system failure.

10. Demonstrated performance: Unless the technology or software is one of a kind, or new to the market, there are likely existing programs or companies that may provide valuable insights into their experience with all nine of the preceding selection factors. If a list of users is not immediately available, often the technology or software company providing the product will supply a list of references.

Yet, as the list of selection factors likely suggests, making a judicious selection is not simply a matter of checking the boxes.

Placing the Selection Criteria in Perspective

As Senator Stanford had predicted at Promontory Summit, railroads continued to expand across the United States and the intermountain west. Some 150 years after he had pounded in the golden spike, in April 2012, the Colorado Department of Transportation (CDOT) commissioned a study to examine the feasibility of establishing a 100+-mile high-speed transit system across the Mountain Corridor from Vail to Golden, CO. The study, which solicited proposals from approximately a dozen high-tech firms, was sponsored by the I-70 Coalition, a nonprofit organization comprised of 26 counties, towns, and resorts along the proposed rail line routes whose collective mission was "to enhance public accessibility and mobility . . . through the implementation of public and private transportation management efforts."[9]

Numerous constraints, interfaces, and technical challenges had to be addressed in proposals: tight horizontal and vertical curves; stretches located within or adjacent to undeveloped areas, National Forest land

and Wilderness Areas—all requiring U.S. Forest Service permits; high elevations and steep grades; and potential construction or destruction of up to 35 tunnels.

As the request for proposal made note, the stakeholders were particularly inclined to the introduction of new technologies: "a successful outcome may set the standard of expectations for High-Speed Rail in the western United States."[10] In addition to the multiple technology options the request was expected to solicit, the CDOT indicated four potential routes bidders could propose.

Acceptance criteria for proposals introduced rigorous challenges for prospective bidders: achieving design speeds up to 180 miles/hour, allowing the route, including up to six stops, to be completed in approximately one hour; accommodating grades up to 7 percent; operating in all winter conditions; ensuring passenger, vehicle, and system safety; and utilizing proven and available technologies that either had "commercial availability, and/or [were] subject to full-size independent evaluation by the end of 2017."[11]

Were the challenges not sufficient, encouraging the development of new technologies, it was recognized, came with its own set of potential risks. Therefore, to provide for a level of confidence that bidders could deliver on the technologies they proposed, the CDOT established a robust technology readiness classification logic. Bidders were required to delineate the precise status of development for each technology proposed as a means of meeting the established acceptance criteria. Technologies judged not to be sufficiently advanced to meet the 2017 delivery date would be reason to reject the proposal.

Being widely applicable to any planned implementation of technologies, these readiness designations developed by the CDOT are a valuable complement to the other technology selection criteria just discussed (Table 3.1).[12]

After 28 months (in August 2014), the completed feasibility study was finally issued. Unfortunately, the price tags (just for the capital expenditures) in the proposals ranged from $5.5 to $13.4 billion. Being that the total budget for the State of Colorado at the time was $24 billion and the CDOT budget was only $1.1 billion, the feasibility study offered a significantly understated conclusion that "allocating state funds . . . would be difficult."

Table 3.1 Degrees of technology readiness

	Stage of Development	How Characterized
1	Basic principles observed and reported	Scientific research just entering the development stage; no actual testing yet conducted
2	Technology concept and/or application formulated	Application of the technology is speculative. Activity is shifting from pure research to applied research, with particular focus on the proposed application
3	Component and/or initial validation in laboratory environment	Active research such as analytical studies or examining the integration of components is underway
4	Component and/or initial validation in laboratory environment	Basic components of the proposed technology are integrated to confirm that they will work together, but within a controlled and confined environment
5	Component and/or initial validation in relevant environment	The basic technological components are integrated with supporting and interconnected elements to test the technology in a reasonably simulated (but generally small-scale) environment
6	System/subsystem model or prototype demonstration in a relevant environment	Representative model or prototype system is tested in an environment approximating the anticipated usage and operational requirements; at this stage, development may be considered for initial acceptance
7	System prototype demonstration in an operational environment	A prototype, near or at planned operational capability, is demonstrated in an environment approximating the actual planned application
8	Actual system completed and qualified through test and demonstration	Technology is proven to work in its final form and under expected conditions—essentially completing development. Completion of this phase allows for introducing the technology into the actual system where it will be tested and evaluated
9	Actual system proven through successful deployment	Once installed in the actual operating environment, technology is confirmed in its final form, under actual operational conditions, and at design capacities. Operational testing and evaluation establish documented proof of performance satisfying all acceptance criteria

As the feasibility study elaborated: "As of 2014, there are no local, state, or federal funds currently available for an AGS [Advanced Guideway System] for the I-70 Mountain Corridor, and therefore the AGS is not financially feasible at this time."[13] Although the study demonstrated that "technologies exist that can exceed the AGS performance and operational criteria," nothing was going to be constructed.

Seeking to place a positive spin on the two-year investment in the study, later that year the 2014 *Annual Report* from the CDOT Division of Transit and Rail highlighted the fact that "the studies show that a . . . system could provide many benefits to the businesses, individuals, and tourists that depend on Colorado's interstate corridors."[14]

Despite the modest value of proving the technical concept and documenting assorted future benefits to the various communities, the question to be asked was evident: Was the 2+-year study truly worth it for any of the engaged and interested parties: stakeholders, bidders, the CDOT, or the commercial interests along the Mountain Corridor?

If you consider the Mountain Corridor communities, it's hard to reconcile the time and expense with the value gained. The sponsors of the feasibility study (the I-70 Coalition) and all the regional stakeholders whose aspirations were to set a new transportation standard received nothing at the time or for the foreseeable future by which "to enhance public accessibility and mobility."

Although it is not known how much it cost each of the bidders to develop a proposal responsive to the constraints and acceptance criteria, it is not uncommon for contracts of values equivalent to that of the proposed rail system to cost bidders in excess of $3 million to develop a winning proposal. For all of their efforts and costs, bidders simply proved to themselves that they had the capability to build an AGS—but did not gain the experience or profit from actually constructing one. In other words, they recovered nothing against their financial outlay.

As for the CDOT, the study likely told them what they already knew before the study began: (1) technologies were available (otherwise they would not have been able to identify a dozen credible and capable bidders) and (2) given its mandated scope of responsibility, the CDOT certainly could have projected a rough order of magnitude cost per mile that would have made evident that funding for the initiative did not exist anywhere or any time soon in the Colorado budgets.

The lesson—other than providing us with an effective means for evaluating technology readiness—is that the criteria for selecting new technologies or automating processes need not always require extensive analysis. Rather, as was the logic employed when we were assembling our initial process improvement team, reliance on reason has to be one of the prime mechanisms contributing to the decision-making process when considering the introduction of new technologies.

In this instance, a simple three-step equation was all that was needed: (1) multiply the average cost per mile to do railroad construction as had been completed elsewhere in the state times the number of miles in the AGS; (2) add in a factor (let's say 20 percent) to account for this project's unique constraints and relatively young technology; and then (3) compare that total estimated cost with the sum of projected available state funds plus the projected income from operating the spur for the first 5 to 10 years. That basic equation would have made the significant delta between cost and funding readily apparent, either negating the need for endorsing two years of intense analysis or, at minimum, providing the basis for recasting the aspirations.

And if one party engaged in the decision making were to propose proceeding with putting the proposals together and having them ready to go if and when funding became available, two major weaknesses in that reasoning would also have been made apparent. First, proceeding with development of proposals still saddled the bidders with an unrecovered financial liability. Even if all variables, constraints, and interfaces remained constant between the time proposals were submitted and the funding became available (which is highly improbable), by law, being that there is government funding involved, a whole new competitive bidding cycle with new proposals would have been required. Second, unless the funding materialized in the following two or maybe three years (at most) following submission of proposals, it's likely that further advances in technology subsequent to submission of the proposals would have introduced better, safer, and cheaper means of delivering the desired Mountain Corridor service.

This cautionary tale of committing resources far in excess of what might be needed to make a reasonable decision about selecting technology suggests why it is not enough to simply identify the appropriate criteria to apply. Criteria should be prioritized and, focusing on the factors of highest priority (e.g., cost, schedule, and operability), a preliminary determination made on whether any or all of the most significant criteria suggest a clear-cut answer to whether the prudent path is to proceed with a more detailed technology evaluation or to recast the proposed action.

As this caution suggests, there are other risks that may come into play when introducing technology. Although not necessarily formal selection criteria, assessing these risks is useful in informing the selection criteria—assisting in characterizing the reasonableness of the investment or giving a sense of magnitude to both benefits and shortcomings.

In particular, there are 10 risks that routinely prove relevant to the process of selecting technology:

- Architecture: The new technology does not adequately support the program owing to misalignments between technologies already in use and the proposed technologies.
- Audit: Evaluations conducted during the course of the selection process do not accurately assess design or operational elements of the technology.
- Availability: Not only is there a question of the commercial availability of the technology or software; a factor that must be considered is the availability of resources to implement, operate, and maintain the technology or software.
- Budget: Although the initial funding may be sufficient, the budget to support the technology over its lifetime (e.g., licenses, upgrades, maintenance, and replacement) needs to be evaluated to ensure that the strategic implications have all been considered.
- Capacity: Projections on the company's potential growth or expansion may factor into the determination of whether continued sufficient capacity will exist for both short- and long-term needs. Like a school district that builds a high school but underestimates the area's student population growth, inappropriately sizing capacity may introduce more long-term insufficiency than efficiency.
- Change control: The company must have a system by which to record and capture changes and modifications to the technology as they occur. Losing sight of changes places jeopardy on the continued efficiency and operation

of technology and software. Also, as we noted, the extent of customization translates directly into issues when upgrades to technology or software occur: Each aspect of local tailoring of the configuration represents additional support or programming when equipment or software updates are provided.

- Facility and infrastructure needs: Analysis must consider physical requirements such as space required, power, network reliability, and computing capabilities.

- Operational lifetime: Depending on the technology, there may be issue with its longevity, the duration of technical support from the technology's manufacturer, and long-term availability of replacement hardware or software.

- Personnel acceptance: Automating and introducing technology is often accompanied by changes that may be seen by the workforce as adversely affecting personnel. For example, automation may contribute to a reduction in staffing or reassignment of personnel. The impacts may cause resentment of management and resistance to the successful implementation of the technology.

- Vendor reliability: As we discussed in the case of the CDOT's quest to introduce a high-speed rail system, the question must be considered about the state of the technology—whether it exists commercially, has been proven in an equivalent operational environment, or, rather, is still in some stage of development or pending adaptation to the proposed market.

In the end, the only reliable means by which to assure that the decision to move forward with a particular technology or automation initiative is in fact a prudent step is by assiduously applying the selection criteria, whether evaluating a single piece of technology or trying to determine the best fit from among several options.

As the CDOT example laid out, it is also a good idea—when appropriate—to include an option of not introducing any technology in the evaluation. Years ago, the U.S. government learned that using a "do nothing" option in Environmental Impact Statements was a helpful means to ensure all perspectives were considered prior to authorizing activities that would affect protected land areas. Barring the inclusion of a "no action" alternative, as the U.S. government learned, can result in a poor (or inappropriate) selection simply because the option selected is the best available from among the presented alternatives—not because it is the "best" or most appropriate course of action.

As has been our approach with the use of the Toulmin model and the process flowchart, capturing and evaluating the bases for technology selection decisions is also best accomplished through a simple record. In this instance, we make evident how the decision was reached by using a form that prioritizes the selection criteria cited earlier, ranks technology choices against those criteria, and also incorporates notations regarding risks that apply to any of the technology options. Also, as we noted, the form includes a ranking for a course of taking no action, that is, foregoing the introduction of new technology or software (Figure 3.4).

Implementing Technology

Having reached a decision on what technology to apply, the effort shifts to its implementation. Here, too, the process must be disciplined and deliberate.

As was suggested in the discussion of the CDOT's pursuit of a high-speed rail system to service the Mountain Corridor, there are a number of major steps in the process of delivering a new technology solution. Whereas the CDOT concentrated exclusively on technical feasibility (which kept the focus principally on selection), had they proceeded to procure and implement the technology, they would have been engaged in four principal phases—as is the case with all technology initiatives.

1. Scoping and test strategy: In this phase, a technical evaluation team is chartered and begins its work by gaining full appreciation of the background, expectations, and requirements for the technological solution. Using this information, the evaluation team develops a project summary detailing the objectives and scope and then performs a market survey to identify prospective vendors or technology

Technology Proposal: Originator: Rationale:

Selection Factor		Proposed Options for Technology Enhancement					
		Take No Action		Technology Option 1		Technology Option 2	
Criteria	Priority*	Criteria Rating**	Additional Risk Factors	Criteria Rating	Additional Risk Factors	Criteria Rating	Additional Risk Factors
Features			•		•		•
Usability			•		•		•
Security			•		•		•
Flexibility			•		•		•
Interoperability			•		•		•
Innovation			•		•		•
Costs			•		•		•
Public Receptivity			•		•		•
Reg. Compliance			•		•		•
Demonstrated Performance			•		•		•

*Priority Ranking: 1: Essential 2: Beneficial 3: Nice to Have 4: Limited Value 5: Not Applicable

**Criteria Rating: 1: Exceeds acceptance criteria 2: Meets acceptance criteria 3: Marginally acceptable 4: Does not meet acceptance criteria

Figure 3.4 Technology selection ranking form

developers. Once a list of prospective suppliers is finalized, concurrent with issuing solicitations or requests for proposals, the evaluation team prepares test plans prescribing the criteria, methodologies, and protocols to be used to confirm capabilities and technology performance satisfy the established specifications.

2. Test preparation: The testing environment is established including securing any required equipment or infrastructure. Efforts may entail not only technical preparations but also completion of any legal or contractual components, such as signing of nondisclosure agreements (NDAs). Once the technical and contractual framework has been established, the technology to be tested is installed in the test environment.

3. Testing, results, and final report: On completion of testing, products are scored relative to their performance against the testing and acceptance criteria. Critical in this phase is that all testing of alternative technologies is performed under identical conditions. Testing continues until all aspects of the test plans have been completed and documented, including notation regarding relevant communications among the supplier, evaluation team, and company technical resources during the course of testing. Findings are compiled into a final report and reviewed with the procuring organization. If established in the contractual agreements, performance of a company's product may also be reviewed with the owner of the technology.

4. Integration and deployment: A final evaluation report is submitted to the procuring department. If a purchase or lease agreement is reached, the appropriate resources (from the procuring company, the vendor, or a separate subcontracted entity) assist in deploying and integrating the solution into the operational environment. During this phase, all appropriate documentation is incorporated into the company's information management system. Operational documents (e.g., procedures and maintenance instructions) are also prepared; at the same time, the associated training, as we will be discussing in the next chapter, is designed and completed. Figure 3.5 provides a basic flowchart of the process of implementation.

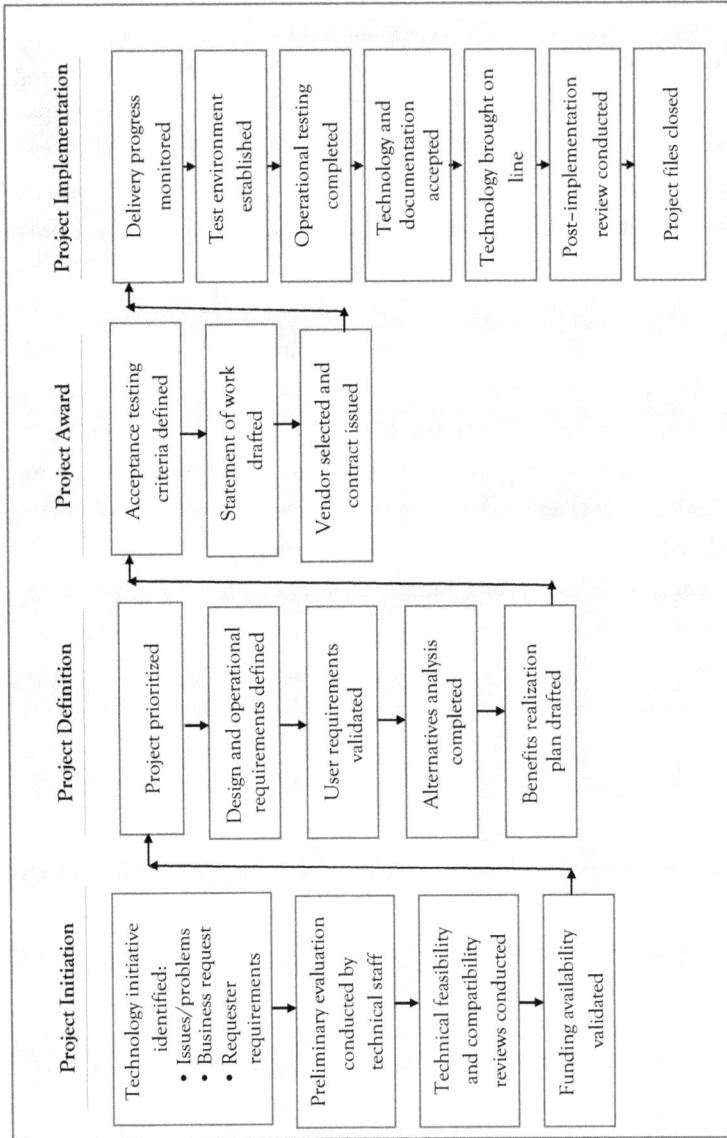

Figure 3.5 Summary technology process

Technology in Perspective

Before we move on to other categories of enrichment and optimization, it would be appropriate to return momentarily to Dr. Calver (and indirectly to Senator Stanford). As we noted parenthetically about Dr. Calver's helio-motor, he and his time lacked the superconducting materials essential for the unimpeded transmission of the energy he was attempting to harness. However, it was almost coincident in time with the popularization of Calver's efforts that attention to his missing component, the concept of superconductivity, emerged.

In 1911, a Dutch physicist, Heike Onnes, observed that at an extremely low temperature (–452°F)—a point referred to as the critical temperature in physics—mercury loses all its electrical resistance. This phenomenon, which allows a current to pass through without diminishing its strength, he named "superconductivity."

A decade or two after Dr. Onnes's discovery, another property of superconductors added to their attractiveness as candidates for providing the world with low-cost energy: Superconductors repel magnetic fields, a property known as diamagnetics. The force created in repelling a magnetic field can suspend objects or electrical currents, creating both a resistant-free and frictionless field in which to transmit energy—a "perfect" transmission of energy.

Over the century or so since Dr. Onnes' discovery, a dozen metals have been demonstrated to exhibit the property of superconductivity. However, despite the sought-after means to take advantage of superconductors and their inherent properties, critical temperatures remain in excess of several hundred degrees below zero and therefore have precluded use of superconductors outside of limited and specially equipped environments such as laboratories.

Even with the recent development of high-temperature superconductor (HTS) materials, elements that achieve superconductivity at temperatures significantly warmer than previously required, commercialization remains on an extremely small scale and limited to a handful of medical and research applications (e.g., nuclear magnetic resonance (NMR) machines and particle accelerators).

And yet, while generally restricted to modest applications, superconductivity is being explored as the basis for one large-scale application that would have been enthusiastically applauded by both Senator Stanford and the CDOT: super speed railways. In Japan, two rail lines are being constructed—between Tokyo and Nagoya and between Tokyo and Osaka (scheduled for completion in 2027 and 2045, respectively). The $55 billion "meglev" (magnetic levitation) train system will use superconductivity to lift the train, keep it centered within the guideway, and move it forward. Traveling at speeds upwards of 500 km/hr (300 miles/hr), the train trip from Tokyo to Nagoya (~352 km) 210 miles will take 40 minutes; Tokyo to Osaka (~501 km) 311 miles less than an hour.[15]

Somewhat facetiously, this contemporary pursuit of the ultimate energy source might suggest Calver had been aiming in precisely the wrong direction: While Calver was heating things up with the help of the sun and hoping the force capable of melting wrought iron would become the means of fueling America's energy needs, his contemporaries were beginning a century-long journey in search of the means by which to cool those same metals down to temperatures capable of conveying energy.

Stated from a different perspective, it could be argued that, ultimately, both camps were seeking a means to warm things up. Calver was promoting energy delivery by means of seeking maximum achievable temperatures. The generations of researchers succeeding his contemporaries were pursuing the means to achieve sustainable and practical critical temperatures.

Although quite an oversimplification, the summarization does suggest one more important theme applicable to our discussion of technology. When proceeding with the introduction of new technologies, companies must recognize that technologies, proven or not, may, from one company to the next, produce different degrees of success in meeting performance expectations.

The reason for a degree of unpredictability, as we have been emphasizing, is that every commercial setting is somewhat unique: Constraints, variations, interfaces, strategies, and operating environments are distinct to each company, and, potentially, may be distinct even as regards processes and applications within a single company (as was demonstrated in our example of the multiple corporate locations engaged in standardizing the process of receipt control).

However, a less-than-ideal performance should not dissuade a company from pursuing technological opportunities. On the contrary, although an ideal outcome cannot be guaranteed, using the analysis and selection process just discussed provides a high level of confidence that significant (if not 100 percent) projected benefits associated with simplifying, standardizing, and increasing system performance will be realized.

Yet, achieving less than the maximum forecasted benefit is not in and of itself a bad thing. As Tomas Edison remarked: "Just because something doesn't do what you planned, doesn't mean it's useless." There is equal likelihood that the technology introduced will provide enhancements beyond those originally forecast. Or, as is sometimes the case, the benefits may occur in unanticipated aspects of the company.

In that regard, if we evaluate Calver's technological efforts using a broadened perspective (i.e., other than his project being cast as either a 100 percent success or a 100 percent failure), we might better appreciate his efforts. The common characterization that Dr. Calver's invention was a monumental failure is a consequence of grading it against the immodest fanfare that accompanied its arrival. The helio-motor, cast as the answer to all energy needs, was promoted as a technological marvel that no energy source or system (steam, coal, nuclear power, or HTSs) has come close to, nor is likely ever of, achieving.

In contrast, positioned in a different context and assigned a more temperate expectation, Calver's story might have been categorized much differently. Instead of seeing the helio-motor in isolation as a failed attempt to produce the ultimate energy solution, Calver's work might, in fact, be more correctly understood as a minor step in the long chain of developments ultimately leading to the commercialization of solar energy.

In the centuries following Archimedes' use of bronze's reflective powers to set Roman ships on fire, cultures as diverse as the Romans and the Anasazi Indians were building south-facing structures to capture the heat of the sun. By the 19th century, in the decades immediately preceding Dr. Calver's invention, photovoltaics contributed to production of solar-powered engines and water heaters. In this lengthy history of pursing and harnessing power from the sun, the 20th century saw quick progression from passive solar-powered buildings common in the years after WW II to solar cells that continue to become increasingly more efficient at converting sunlight into electricity.

And just as Archimedes has been in the background of many of these advances, so—albeit to a lesser degree—has Dr. Calver. His concepts, as suggested in a patent issued in 1975 for a "Solar Energy Conversion System" (U.S. 3,924,624), remain of value. Reminiscent of Calver's work, the 1975 patent, issued in the height of the commercialization of solar power, described:

> a solar energy concentrator system which includes a centrally dis-
> posed column supporting a solar receiver . . . mounted [on a piv-
> oting platform of] solar reflective elements . . . which are arranged
> to tilt about the axis and . . . thereby direct reflected solar energy
> upon the solar receiver.[16]

Only two U.S. patents were listed in the "References Cited" section of the "Solar Energy Conversion System" patented in 1975: an 1894 patent for an invention "to focus the sun's rays" and Patent Number 260,657, Dr. William Calver's 1882 patent, "Method of and Means for Utilizing the Rays of the Sun."

CHAPTER 4

Crafting Personnel Pathways

If you only learn the methods, you'll be tied to your methods, but if you learn the principles, you can devise your own methods.

—Ralph Waldo Emerson

In 1988, Dick Wolf, a Hollywood screenwriter, developed a concept for a television series about the American criminal justice system. Each episode, based on real events, would employ a two-part structure: Part 1 would follow two New York detectives investigating violent crimes; Part 2 would portray the prosecution of the criminals. Unsuccessfully marketed to Fox and CBS, a single season of the show was purchased by NBC. On September 13, 1990, "Prescription for Death," Season 1, Episode 1 of *Law and Order* was broadcast.

In that episode, a man alleges that his daughter who had gone to the emergency room had been murdered. Prompted by the accusation, an investigation is launched. The detectives' suspicion of a cover-up sparked by a less than forthcoming staff is confirmed by an incomplete and doctored medical chart. The investigation concludes an impaired doctor's negligence caused the girl's death. With charges filed, the Assistant District Attorney is challenged to deliver a trial strategy that can succeed against an acclaimed doctor and a venerable institution as defendants.

Following the show's blueprint, "Prescription for Death" was based on an actual case that occurred a few years earlier at New York Hospital, a hospital that has the distinction of being the third oldest hospital in the nation and the second oldest in years of continuous operation.

A New York City landmark, New York Hospital, now part of the Presbyterian Hospital System, was granted a royal charter by King George III in 1771 and convened its first board of governors' meeting at Bolton's Tavern, the same location where General George Washington a few years later would bid farewell to his officers following conclusion of the American Revolution. After a series of construction delays, largely owing to the Revolution, in 1791, New York Hospital opened its doors for "reception of such patients as require medical treatment, surgical management and maniacs."[1] Over centuries of operation, the hospital has remained a leader in providing quality medical care.

One substantive challenge to that reputation occurred in March 1984 when an 18-year-old college student named Libby Zion arrived at the emergency room suffering from fever, chills, and flu-like symptoms. She was examined and admitted by an intern who was eight months out of medical school and a junior resident who had one additional year of training. Notified two hours later by the nurses that the patient was restless and agitated, the intern—who didn't personally check on the woman—had her restrained and ordered a sedative.

The sedative, adversely interacting with prescription medications she had identified while providing her medical history, caused her temperature to spike to 107°F followed quickly by cardiac arrest and death. Her death, publicized as a case of negligence by her father, resulted in several members of the hospital staff being subject to investigation by the state board of medical examiners, a grand jury hearing, and, in 1994, a civil trial—inquiries that highlighted the frequency of residents' medical errors and issues with their training.

As cited in a 2016 issue of the *BMJ* (formerly the *British Medical Journal*), researchers estimated that 10 percent (>250,000) of U.S. deaths each year are due to medical error, making it at the time the third highest cause of death. A primary response, the researchers noted, was the need to develop "consensus protocols" for the practice of medicine.[2]

Over several decades, Libby Zion's death remained a lingering component of the "consensus protocols" debate. As one research article succinctly summarized: the "circumstances that led to the death of Libby Zion in 1984 brought to the national forefront discussions about the impact of resident fatigue on patient outcomes."[3]

Medical student apprenticeships (or residencies) in the United States date back to Johns Hopkins University in 1897. As instituted there, "residents truly resided in the hospital. They received little or no pay, were discouraged from marriage, and worked 24 hours a day, 7 days a week, 365 days a year."[4] Despite studies in the 1970s that demonstrated "serious medical errors [occurred] when they [residents] worked frequent shifts of twenty-four hours or more," work requirements for residents at the time of Libby Zion's death and for 20+ years thereafter routinely entailed 36-hour shifts and on-call assignments comprising up to 130 hours in a week.[5]

To improve patient care, in 1987, the New York State Department of Health issued formal controls for the training of interns and residents. Popularly known as the Libby Zion Act, it set 80 as the maximum total number of working hours per week; limited shifts to no more than 24 consecutive hours; and required at least one period of 24-hours off each week.

The medical community vigorously opposed imposition of these guidelines arguing that any limitation diminished the effectiveness and thoroughness of residents' training. "It would be unrealistic to expect residents to absorb the realities of caring for their equally fragile and needy patients if their working hours were fixed according to an arbitrary schedule, however well-intended."[6] Holding firm to this assertion, it was not until 2003, 16 years after New York enacted the Libby Zion Act that the agency responsible for accrediting medical residency programs finally issued comparable guidelines.

As we have been discussing in the preceding chapters, in businesses and industrial environments, operation of complex processes may require detailed procedures and protocols; programs often rely on a network of constraints, variations, and interfaces; and technology periodically redefines the scope and approaches to conducting work.

As a consequence, the complexity of the business environment often requires multiple (sometimes segregated) disciplines to operate efficiently, for example, accountants in finance, engineers in research, electricians to provide facility and maintenance support, and technicians to operate production lines. As just these examples suggest, the right mix of capabilities, skills, educational demands, and experience may vary from group to group: Engineers and accountants are generally expected to have completed years of formal study; mechanics are hired based on practical experience gained in trade schools and on-the-job training; and technicians may be hired based on general competencies that align with the tasks they will be assigned to perform.

It is with this backdrop that the Libby Zion story provides meaningful perspective on the key dimensions for a complete understanding of training. The protracted debate over "consensus protocols" for medical training did not center on issues of the substance or the thoroughness of training; in many regards those are the easiest attributes to assess. Medical training, as the medical communities both for and against regulating work hours agreed, was, by necessity, lengthy, intense, and demanding.

Whereas the expectations for most working disciplines emphasize either training or education, medical training fuses the concepts together: As a prerequisite to practicing, doctors must complete numerous years of intensive formal study; obtain extensive hands-on experience; and undergo rigorous and highly supervised training on the relevant practices, procedures, and skills.

By straddling the lines between education and training, the Libby Zion story not only correctly broadens the concept of training as it applies to business (encompassing what are generally considered in business as two separate pathways—training and education), but also, at the same time, keenly focuses our attention on the fundamentals and challenges of defining, delivering, and assessing effectiveness of training.

Education Versus Training

Most commonly, especially in larger corporations, training and education (or professional development) are considered two different and separate functions—targeted at different communities and provided by different staffs. Training is principally focused on task-specific activities associated with generating the company's deliverables and product lines; professional development focuses on education-based career enhancement, with support addressed to (but not necessarily required of) those aspects of the business populated by degreed personnel.

In reality, such a dichotomy is arbitrary and mischaracterized. The complexities of modern industry preclude an absolute segregation of training from education. Whether a junior operator on a production line or a senior engineer with some esoteric specialization, maintaining the quality of day-to-day performance necessitates both training and education.

Even if we use the military as example, a model many might assume (as articulated in an opinion published in a 1995 issue of *Army Times*) is among the most likely work environments completely to separate training from education, we cannot escape the overlap. As the author of that opinion espoused, "enlisted soldiers do not have to be degree-toting, highly educated folks. . . . The job of enlisted soldiers is to perform the tasks required to get the job done in accordance with the orders and policies of their commanding officer."[7] The premise of that opinion was summarily dismissed by the director of Servicemembers Opportunity Colleges (an agency that assists service members with pursuing their educational benefits):

> The nation needs servicemembers who are both educated and trained. The way military force is used these days in highly charged and complex "peacetime" politico-military environments clearly requires more than a military man or woman narrowly attuned to a combat task.[8]

Momentarily returning to the Revolutionary War provides the historical context by which to judge these divergent opinions. It was the Founding Fathers' intention that the country's defense would be best served in the hands of citizen-soldiers, trained by the military but educated in civil society. This complementary status of training and education had its genesis during the winter of 1778 where, at Valley Forge, General George Washington directed his chaplain to teach soldiers to read—a philosophy and tradition sustained through generations and formalized with the creation of the Army Continuing Education System some 200 years later. As the Director of Education for the Headquarters Department of the Army wrote at the time: "Education enhances training and develops better soldiers . . . . education should be integrated with training programs."[9]

In keeping with this acknowledgement that education and training are inextricably tied, our discussion will, for simplicity's sake, continue to refer to all efforts at personnel enhancement as "training," but with the intent that the term represents the collective components of both training and education. As such, for our purposes, the stipulated definition of training is the investment in professional development designed

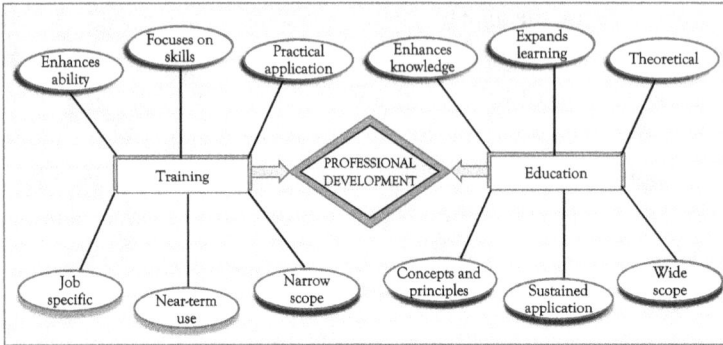

Figure 4.1 The elements of professional development

to better equip all personnel to perform more effectively, more efficiently, and more productively irrespective of job assignment, credentials, or position title (Figure 4.1).

The Essentials of Effective Training

The actual training process can be divided into three major segments: the determination of training needs, the design and delivery of the training, and an evaluation process that considers both the quality and the effectiveness of the materials and the degree to which the training has resulted in the desired change in knowledge and performance (Figure 4.2).

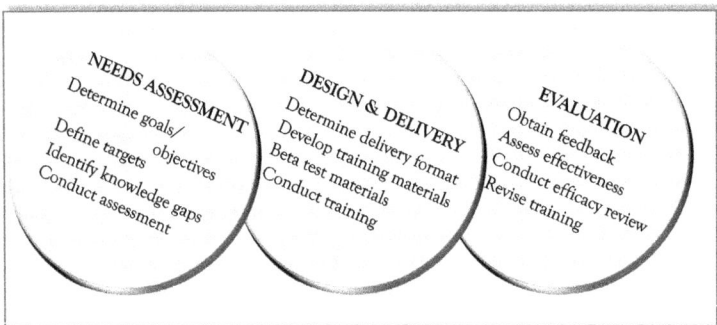

Figure 4.2 The three-step training process

Determining Training Needs

Based on the circumstances, there are numerous means of determining training needs. The most fundamental questions that need to be answered prior to initiating such an assessment involve understanding why the training is being undertaken, the source of the request, and, to the degree feasible, understanding what is to be accomplished (i.e., what would constitute success at the conclusion of the training).

The "why training" question helps to define both the scope and the substance of the training. Training, for instance, intended to prepare individuals for new assignments takes on a different focus than, let's say, training to perform new or revised procedures. The second question (who initiated the training) is of consequence in understanding such factors as the level of resources likely to be provided, the corporate context for the training, and whether the effort is localized or has a broad implication. The last question, and the one frequently overlooked or oversimplified, is what outcome the training is supposed to produce.

The reason this last question is of significance is that without a predefined measure of success, too many training efforts simply assume completing the presentation is synonymous with success—relying on trainee feedback sheets that focus on their satisfaction with the material and instructor competency. Yet neither of these concerns is indicative of the achieved or sustained value of the training. A related problem occurs when training objectives are laid out but are generalized, focused more acutely on what is to be presented than on the intent of the sessions.

Instead, to be effective, the training goals need to deal directly with the first question that precipitated the training: Why is the training needed? The goals should demonstrate how the training satisfies the initiating purposes. The goals should reflect the company's perspective—not the students' expectations, a statement of the scope of the training, or attention to the instructor or the delivery methods. To this end, Table 4.1 provides a basic synopsis of the various approaches to conducting the training needs analyses, their applications, and their primary considerations.

Table 4.1 Forms of training needs analysis

Training-Related Analyses	General Focus	Initiating Condition	Defining Elements/Focal Areas and Objectives
Organizational analysis	Company strategies, goals, or objectives	• Management concern regarding overall company performance	• Clear definition of precisely what the company sees as success/high performance • Availability and effectiveness of training resources
Person-specific analysis	Individuals identified as requiring training	• New/revised procedures • New processes, technology • Individual performance • New/advancement opportunities	• Individuals' current credentials and the expected credentials posttraining • Appropriate delivery mechanisms
Work/task analysis	Evaluating the means by which activities are completed	• Specific changes in how the company operates (encompassing operational, administrative, technical, and management levels)	• Understanding the skill level or knowledge expected to perform tasks effectively
Performance analysis	Opportunities to enhance overall effectiveness, quality, or productivity	• Performance levels indicating negative trends or below expectations or projections • Enhanced performance targets	• Evaluation of the contributors to performance • Degree of improvement anticipated • Assessment of delivery options
Training content/design analysis	Identification of the skills and education warranted to meet position requirements and expectations	• Performance is assumed to be constrained by poor controls or disconnect between the activity and the credentials of the assigned individuals • Controls not effectively designed	• Controls effectively aligned with safety, quality, technical, and performance expectations • Design, availability, and use of controls • Training provided on procedures and protocols
Training suitability analysis	Is training the appropriate solution to bring performance up to expectations?	• Training costs or time are not aligned with the demands of the position or the assignment • Training appears to be unnecessary, excessive, or redundant	• Does the complexity or the demands of the scope of work warrant training? • How are essential capabilities acquired and demonstrated?
Cost–benefit analysis	Is the company getting its money's worth from training?	• Performance subsequent to training does not indicate anticipated degree of improvement	• What is the training intended to accomplish? • How much value was it intended to add? • What issues are limiting its value?

Beyond potential issues that need to be avoided regarding the setting of the training goals, there are five common mistakes in the assessment of training needs that should be rigorously guarded against:

1. Not engaging management: Both the management that initiated the training and the management of the training attendees need to remain actively engaged. Without management's explicit attention and endorsement, personnel are quick to assume the training is not of great consequence or is a short-term fix for a problem which they may not see as urgent.

2. Not allowing sufficient time: Conducting a thorough training needs analysis is a function of putting in sufficient time to ascertain all the dimensions contributing to the need for training and to do the appropriate research and preplanning. As with many assignments, the upfront planning effort can be more taxing and time consuming than the actual development or delivery of the training.

3. Using out-of-date information: Training may be repetitive, delayed, or phased. Whatever the circumstance, the training must be current. Update any materials that had been used previously, were prepared far in advance of the training, or may rely on outdated references, sources, or examples. Training that isn't current may not only be limited in its applicability but also reduce both the benefits and the credibility of the training.

4. Arbitrarily shortcutting the research: As a corollary to providing sufficient time for the analysis, make certain all relevant resources are reviewed when constructing the analysis. As appropriate, planning should consider first-hand observations of group interactions as well as actual performance of work; should consider interviews or small group conversations with management, affected personnel, and representatives from programs that can provide insights; and reflect careful review of relevant documents as well as any previously provided training with a similar or related focus. Both the quality and credibility of the analysis are contingent on the research's completeness, accuracy, and currency.

5. Assuming training is always the best resolution of a training or knowledge gap: As suggested by the suitability analysis (Table 4.1),

training is not always the best or only solution to resolving a knowledge or performance gap. However, a comprehensive training needs assessment is among the most effective tools in determining the best course to close that gap—the right approach, attendees, scope, delivery methodology, and evaluative techniques.

As we had discussed when exploring the process for selecting and evaluating new technologies, this phase in the training process—completing the training needs analysis—is the point at which training personnel and management can most fully grasp the complete picture of the magnitude and nature of any performance or knowledge gap, define precisely what is needed to close that gap, and authorize the most effective means by which to accomplish that goal.

Designing and Delivering Training

Too often training focuses immediately on the matter of designing and creating materials—slides, handouts, exercises. However, just as careful attention must be paid to maintaining a focus on the theme and purpose of the material, so the design must begin with the definition of a communication strategy—how best to present the material to ensure it is understood and the imparted knowledge is retained. Intending to accomplish these two components of successful training—knowledge delivery and retention—often leads to discussion of learning theory. Reviews of adult learning theories make evident that there are numerous ways in which people learn:

- Behaviorism = Learning results in response to an external stimulus.
- Cognitivism = Learning results from internalizing concepts and information.
- Constructivism = Learning results from adding new knowledge to existing modes of thinking.
- Experiential = Learning results from interaction with one's environment.

- Humanistic = Learning is driven by a goal of personal improvement.
- Motivational = Learning is promoted by a need to succeed or attain a goal.
- Reflective = Learning derives from rethinking responses and modes of thinking.
- Social = Learning occurs from adopting observed behaviors or modes of thinking.
- Transformative = Learning occurs from successfully challenging beliefs or modes of thinking.

As valuable as these learning theories may be in certain contexts, as we laid out in the Introduction, one of our principles is to maintain a practical orientation, with "tools and techniques that can be applied with minimal training or facilitation by those individuals." Just as we identified the methodology developed by Stephen Toulmin as a means to effectively assess evaluating the appropriateness of judgments and team decisions, so there is a practical means to establish a common denominator approach that captures the implicit logic underpinning the many learning theories.

A behavioral scientist at Stanford, and founder of the university's Behavior Design Lab, B.J. Fogg developed an insightful approach that synthesizes such factors as environment, experiences, and goals into a simple framework that, as he asserts, "has special relevance to those of us who study and design persuasive technology."[10] In a complement to Toulmin's model that depicted the elements of arguments, the Fogg Behavior Model, as it has come to be called, can assist in developing the design of materials that promote effective training.

As professor Fogg noted,

The tools for creating persuasive products are getting easier to use, with innovations in online video, social networks, and metrics, among others. As a result, more individuals and organizations can design experiences they hope will influence people's behaviors via technology channels. However, many attempts at persuasive design fail because people don't understand what factors lead to behavior change.

The Fogg Behavior Model represents the fundamentals of behavior change as a basic equation: Behavior = Motivation + Ability + Trigger. Simply stated, Fogg's concept relies on three assumptions: when highly motivated, people can readily change their behavior; people are most willing to make a change in behavior when the change is something easy to accomplish; and behavioral change is facilitated by applying the right triggers (or prompts) at appropriate times.

As Dr. Fogg explains:

In order for behavior to occur, people must have some non-zero level of both motivation and ability. The implication for designers is clear: Increasing motivation is not always the solution. Often increasing ability (making the behavior simpler) is the path for increasing behavior performance.

The instigating agents for the moments of change are the triggers applied at the opportune moment to persuade.

The first two factors, motivation and ability, can each be adjusted, increasing the likelihood of successfully attaining a new behavior. However, while motivations must be individually determined with each trainee or group of trainees, increasing an employee's ability to change can be positively influenced by adjustments in the training protocols: providing sufficient time for trainees to learn and appreciate the new behavior; ensuring availability of the appropriate resources; ensuring materials and exercises are not overly taxing (either physically or mentally); and promoting behavioral changes in concert with accepted norms and practices.

Triggers, the third element of Fogg's model, can be any initiating notice issued to the trainee that indicates when the behavioral change is to be made or practiced. "Effective persuasive technologies will boost either motivation or ability . . . or both. But that's not all: The behavior must be triggered. This third factor is often the missing piece."

As Dr. Fogg explains, there are three types of triggers: (1) sparks— when motivation is low, this type of trigger prompts the individual to make the change in behavior; (2) facilitators—when motivation is high but ability is low, this trigger makes the behavior easier to attain; and (3) signals—this trigger serves as a reminder whenever the behavior is to be repeated. "Taken together, the three factors . . . become focal areas for persuasive technology. In general, persuasive design focuses on increasing motivation, increasing ability (simplicity), and triggering behavior." Figure 4.3 depicts the interrelationships among motivation, ability, and triggers as suggested in the Fogg Behavior Model.

So, let's examine how the Fogg Behavior Model translates into the design of effective training materials. For the purposes of discussion, assume the upper chart in Figure 4.4 represents attendees' attitudes and performance at the start of a training session. After conducting pretraining interviews with the attendees and management, the perception is that the trainees expect the new training and its associated terminology are going to be difficult to understand; further, they are less than fully motivated owing to the fact that this new training represents the third new technology they have had to master in the last two years.

The bottom chart in Figure 4.4 indicates management's performance expectations consequent to the training: a team suitably knowledgeable

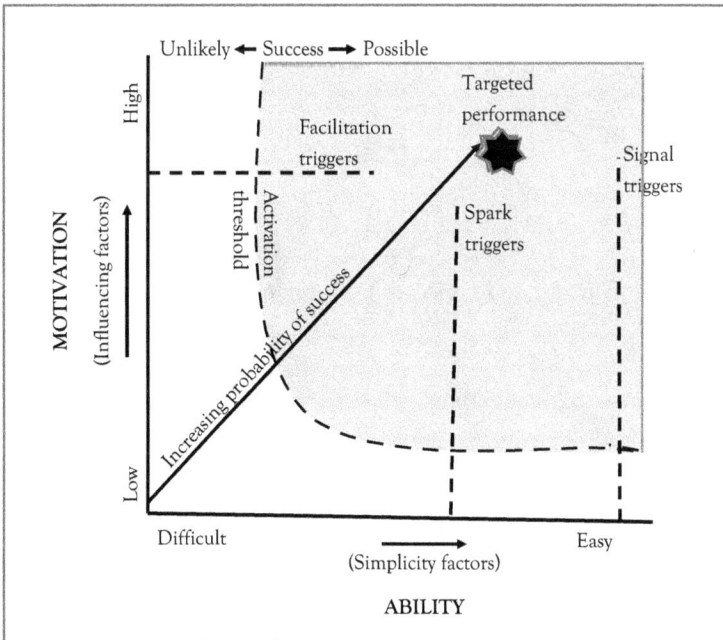

Figure 4.3 Depiction of the elements of the Fogg Behavior Model

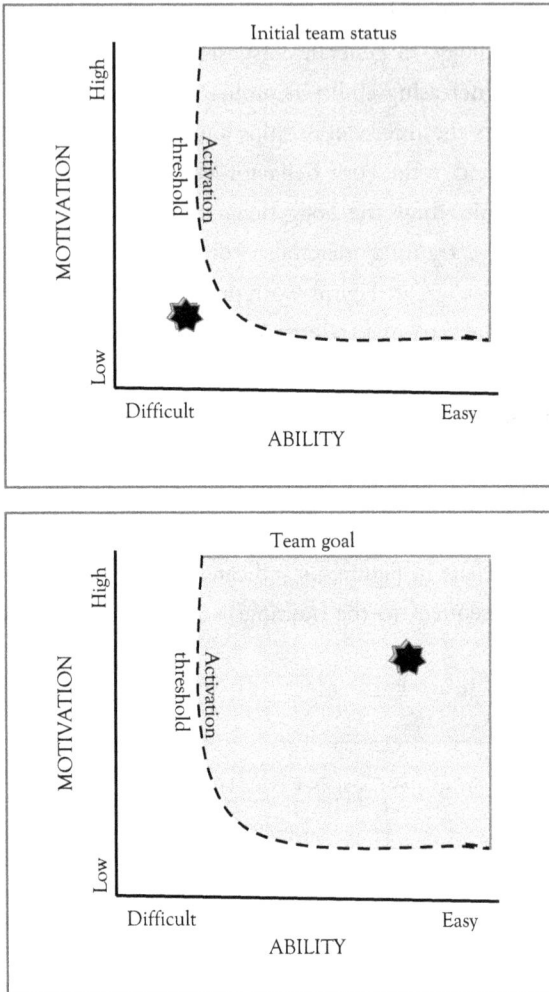

Figure 4.4 Current and projected perceptions of team behaviors

about the new technology, prepared to assume its operation, and support-ive of the ongoing strategic efforts to automate operations throughout the corporation.

Considering motivation and ability challenges anticipated, the train-ing for this team would likely be most effective if it incorporates the types of features indicated in Table 4.2. As the lists in Table 4.2 make evident, one important (and unique) benefit of utilizing the Fogg Behavior Model

Table 4.2 Designing for success

Motivating factors	• Possibilities of promotion based on expanded technical expertise • Bonuses for improved section performance and output consequent to implementing the technology • Active management encouragement at the onset and during the course of the training • Acknowledgement through the company recognition program • Certificates and plaques
Simplicity factors (enhanced ability)	• Techniques taught are shown to be similar to ones already in practice • Information is broken up into small chunks • As information sections are completed, there is hands-on practice sessions • Aids—like illustrated procedures and terminology lists—are provided and routinely referred to during training • Small group exercises are facilitated by experienced operators • Training offered in short sessions (1–2 hours) over the course of several days
Triggers	*Sparks* • Management endorsement and recognition • Teaming with seasoned technicians • Certifications *Facilitating* • Follow up individualized sessions • Mentors assigned • Added time for hands-on practice *Signals* • E-mail notifications highlighting key responsibilities • Schedules posted in work areas • Management reviews • Periodic updates and retraining

when designing training is that the approach extends attention beyond the classroom, lecture hall, or even the field-based elements. Instead, the training design takes into account the full range of techniques and practices needed during and after training to introduce, implement, and sustain the imparted skills, behaviors, and/or knowledge.

Once the motivational framework has been determined, the Fogg Behavior Model can be used as the foundation for an effective instructional strategy. As summarized in the *Harvard Educational Review*, researchers identified a four-step structuring and delivery process that, when practiced by instructors, contributed to student "transformations": "There are ways of talking, showing, enacting, or otherwise representing ideas so that the unknowing can come to know, those without understanding can comprehend and discern, and unskilled can become adept."[11]

This four-step process, which rivals the simplicity of Fogg's insights into behavioral changes, provides the companion methodology that allows the Fogg Behavior Model—motivation factors, simplicity factors, and triggers—to be translated into effective presentation and pedagogical structures:

1. Preparation: critical interpretation and analysis of the available resources, structuring and segmentation of materials, development of the overall delivery plan, and clarification of purposes
2. Representation: determining the means to communicate the concepts and information, for example, analogies, metaphors, examples, demonstrations, hands-on practice, and simulations
3. Selection: defining the instructional strategy—modes of teaching, organizing, managing, and arranging
4. Adapting: tailoring all components to the audience, their perceptions, attitudes, interests, abilities, and motivation[12]

Once the training needs assessment is complete and has been used to define the appropriate training and instructional design, then it is time to initiate the actual production of the training materials. In this final phase of development, the same thoroughness that accompanied the needs assessment and the identification of behavioral and delivery factors must be applied. Pulling the materials together, depending on their complexity, may entail a cast of characters:

- *Project director:* responsible for overall management of the project, setting and maintaining goals and schedules
- *Writers:* responsible for generating text, handouts
- *Media specialist:* responsible for designing audiovisual components of the training
- *Editor:* responsible for the review and final drafts of training materials

- *Illustrator:* responsible for artwork
- *Designer:* responsible for layouts, graphics

All these organizations and individuals should be engaged in both the process of developing and reviewing the quality and appropriateness of the training materials before they are released for use—an activity that can be simplified and monitored by use of a quality checklist (Table 4.3).

Table 4.3 Sample training material quality checklist

Training Alignment	Yes	No	Adjustments Needed
Materials clearly aligned with participants' knowledge and skills gaps?			
Materials presented in a logical and easy-to-follow sequence?			
Materials collectively address management's expectations?			
Training comprehensive enough without being overwhelming?			
Materials include an appropriate selection of tools and techniques?			
Simplicity factors integrated into presentation approach?			
Content			
Clearly presented content?			
Adequate input from content experts?			
Pilot testing conducted and feedback incorporated (if warranted)?			
Appropriate time allotted for each segment of the training?			
Sufficient use of examples, statistics, case studies, etc.?			
Artwork/multimedia materials effectively complement and do not distract from training themes and messages?			
Simplicity factors integrated into the presentation modes?			

(continued)

Table 4.3 (Continued)

Structure			
Logistics (group size, location, facilities) appropriate?			
Access to materials needed for hands-on exercises and practice is readily available (e.g., models, workstations)?			
Time frame allows for accomplishment of all learning activities and tasks?			
Closure tasks (e.g., exams) and evaluation forms developed?			
Posttraining follow-up activities and assignments defined?			
Communication			
Precourse materials and course communications prepared?			
Material structured to be conducive to meaningful exchanges and interactions (during and posttraining)?			
Management engagement and communications lined up?			

Assessing the Effectiveness of Training

In the 1950s, as American industry was ramping up in the years following WW II, interest in understanding the effectiveness of corporate training began growing. As one corporate researcher for B.F. Goodrich noted in a 1957 article published in *Personnel*:

> Managers, . . . expect . . . departments to yield a good return and will go to great lengths to find out whether they have done so. When it comes to training, however, they may expect the return but rarely do they make a like effort to measure the actual results. . . . training directors might be well-advised to take the initiative and evaluate their programs before the day of reckoning arrives.[13]

Among the voices exploring this new area of interest in training effectiveness was that of Donald Kirkpatrick, who, at the time, was the Training Director for the International Minerals and Chemical Corp. Beginning with a series of articles in training-related journals and his 1959 book on *Evaluating Training Programs*, he advocated a four-phased structure for evaluating the effectiveness of training that has become a cornerstone of this field of study.

As he summarized:

Evaluation changes from a complicated elusive generality into clear and achievable goals if we break it down into logical steps. These steps can be defined as follows: Step 1 Reaction. How well did the conferees like the program? Step 2 Learning. What principles, facts and techniques were learned? Step 3 Behavior. What changes in job behavior resulted from the program? Step 4 Results. What were the tangible results of the program in terms of reduced cost, improved quality, improved quantity, etc.?[14]

Over the latter half of his career at the University of Wisconsin, Dr. Kirkpatrick published six more books exploring dimensions of this approach to evaluating training. Over more than half a century, the methodology's very simplicity, practicality, and broad applicability have sustained it as "one of the most recognized project evaluation frameworks."[15] Moreover, its value lies in the fact that it assesses both the informative role of training—the interest in determining means to improve the actual training—and the summative role of training—estimating the program's overall effectiveness.

As one journal article summarized, the Kirkpatrick model

provides one technique for appraisal of the evidence for any reported training program. Moreover, the model can be used to determine whether a favourable outcome is limited to self-reported staff attitudes and practices, or whether there are improvements to relevant knowledge acquisition and application, and even positive impacts on operating costs.

As the article goes on to state:

> The ultimate goal is a training program that will meet the needs of both the staff who will participate and the clients . . . for whom it is intended; but also one that is likely to be implemented by the responsible organisation.[16]

This broad appeal and benefit achieved using Dr. Kirkpatrick's methodology were confirmed in 1997 when the American Society for Training and Development (ASTD) conducted a survey of 300 human resource directors to determine the importance assigned to measuring training effectiveness. More than three-quarters of companies surveyed (81 percent) indicated evaluating training was important, and more than half (67 percent) indicated they used the Kirkpatrick behavior model as their assessment tool.[17]

Reflecting back on the story of Libby Zion, it's worth noting that even the medical profession has come to rely on the Kirkpatrick model in assessing training. In addition to articles citing particular medically related applications of the technique, one 2019 article in *Academic Medicine* used the Kirkpatrick model to evaluate and compare the performance of 21 different medical leadership training programs.[18]

However, before we examine the means to monitor and assess performance against each of the four phases of this evaluation model, Tables 4.4 and 4.5 briefly expand on Dr. Kirkpatrick's methodology. Table 4.4 summarizes the intent of each of the four components and the associated questions that determine whether the intents are being achieved. Table 4.5 provides a brief list of the tools and techniques applicable to each of those four components.

The types of questions to ask and the types of tools to apply are driven by a range of factors identified in the various developmental phases and are determined at each phase of the training: establishing the expectations of the management authorizing the effort; completing the needs analysis, training development, and design phases; and defining the behavioral and instructional elements.

Table 4.4 *Kirkpatrick evaluation model summary*

Reaction	Learning	Behavior	Results
Reaction focuses on the evaluation of the trainees' perception of the training or learning: • Was the training experience positive and relevant? • Was the material easy to understand, easy to follow, and presented effectively? • Was the learning environment (e.g., facilities) conducive to learning? • Was the training worthwhile and did trainees perceive a ready (and sustained) application of the training?	Learning considers the increase in knowledge or performance—generally comparing levels immediately before and after the training: • Did the trainees learn the intended lessons or skills? • How different is the level of performance or knowledge consequent to the training? • Is the level and focus of the advancement consistent with the expectations for the training? • Are there unexpected areas of enhancement?	Behavior concentrates on assessing whether there is a sustained change in behavior (potentially, both short- and long-term): • Is there a sustained and measurable change in the expected behavior on the job? • Does the change in behavior directly affect the intended areas of job performance? • Is the degree of change the same as recorded immediately after training? • Is the trainee aware of the change and able to transfer it to co-workers?	Results examine the implications of the change: i.e., its effect on the business: • Are there gains in production, quality, safety, and profit? • Are there gains in employee satisfaction? • Have there been decreases in process errors, wastage, or customer complaints? • Are the improved behaviors being transferred among the trainees' co-workers? • Do the changes suggest need for additional triggers (Fogg Behavior Model reinforcement)?

Table 4.5 Representative tools for conducting training effectiveness evaluations

Reaction	Learning	Behavior	Results
• Online assessments • Posttraining interviews/questionnaires • Small group feedback sessions held at the conclusion of training • Summary feedback sheets (completed at the end of training or as submitted to the trainee's management)	• Exams • Job proficiency evaluations or formal certifications • Formal or informal assessments • Interviews (of trainees, peers, and management) • Documented observations • Performance reviews	• Trainee surveys • Focused periodic observations • Formal evaluations • Examinations incorporated into routine on-the-job assessment and performance review activities • Feedback from co-workers, management, subordinates	• Metrics tracking quality, safety, production • Interviews with management (particularly managers who authorized the training) • Follow-up small group feedback sessions with trainees • Development and monitoring of specific skills and knowledge gained from training • Annual appraisals

Wrapping Up the Training

With the design and delivery of training completed, the last item to take care of is the record keeping. Because some posttraining activities may go on for some time, or additional training may need to be provided, having a record of what was decided (the planning decisions along with the details of the actual training development, content selection, and design) is an essential piece of the corporate history. To capture the appropriate detail, we generally use a very simple form that requires only essential descriptive notations. The form, in turn, serves as a kind of cover sheet for the training records package, which includes copies of all the pertinent support documentation—copies of conclusions from the needs assessment, course syllabus, and copies of the presentation materials (Figure 4.5).

Transitioning

To this point in our process, the original team that was chartered to revise a process has remained the major driving force in introducing, evaluating, and implementing the associated enhancements in technology and training. The adjustments in technology and training derive directly from the work on the process and are best accomplished through the retention of the personnel who are most familiar with the types of changes and with the rationale and implications (e.g., identification and impacts of variables, constraints, and interfaces).

At this point, the opportunities for broadening the range and magnitude of the enhancements—broadening them from localized improvements into company-wide enhancements—are generally no longer within the range of the initial team's authority or perspective. Achieving the expanded range of enhancement opportunity requires adhering to a simple premise of management: Work is best accomplished when there is alignment among authority, accountability, and responsibility.

When we now reach beyond the localized enhancements and examine the possibilities regarding aspects of the company's structure, its governance, and its business strategies, the determinations and implementation fall to management (and potentially to a board of managers or board of directors).

Training Summary		
Short Title:		Developer:
		Trainer:
Authorizing Manager:		Training Date:
Organization:		
Training Objectives: • • •	• • • • •	
Needs Analysis Activities Completed:		
Previous Related Training:		
Major subject Areas Addressed in Training: • • •	• • •	
Presentation/Delivery Structure:		
Evaluation Tools	Short Term • • •	Long Term • • •

Attachments	Training Aids: ☐	Results of Needs Analysis: ☐
	Syllabus: ☐	Roster: ☐
	Identified Triggers: ☐	Other: ☐

Figure 4.5 Training summary form

Whereas the original team employed people needed to provide the impetus for change in process, technology, and training, organizational changes typically fall to middle management—managers who have responsibility, authority, and accountability for sets of interrelated programs (e.g., engineering, operations, business, and safety). And, when the focus shifts to examination of factors like governance (the overarching corporate protocols and policies) and to the corporate strategies that

Process Design Considerations				Resulting Organizational Initiatives				
Variables	Constraints	Interfaces		Technology	Training	Organizational Realignments	Governance	Strategic Redefinitions
		Functions	Manuals					

Team 1
(Assigned and selected personnel)

Team 2
(Middle management)

Team 3
(Senior management)

Figure 4.6 Column headings for enrichment summary form

governance seeks to enforce, jurisdiction lies exclusively with the company's senior management.

Just as training concluded with a record for use in subsequent developmental efforts, so a report card of sorts is needed to inform the management personnel to whom the next series of corporate-level enhancements fall. But, again, our goal remains simplicity. Managers prefer succinct records explaining what the circumstances are; the principal challenges; what has worked and what has not worked; and why and how decisions were reached.

To this end, as a means to move forward, our initial team completes a record using a basic form—essentially a report card—highlighting the essential aspects of what has been learned and what has been accomplished (Figure 4.6). In specific, the team answers the following questions: What were the variables and the constraints that were addressed when revising the process? What interfacing functions underwent changes as a direct or indirect consequence of the process or technology changes, including what documentations (manuals, procedures, and policies) were issued, revised, or eliminated? What technology was introduced and what were the critical considerations in making the final selection? What training was developed and delivered? How effective has that training proven to be and what controls have been put in place to sustain the achieved gains?

This same form will be used as the efforts shift to issues of organizational alignment, changes in governance, and adjustments in strategies. Using this form as the transformations and enhancements continue by the management team provides a comprehensive record of advances on the road from process improvement to company enrichment.

With completion of their section of this enrichment summary form, the handoff from our original improvement team to management is made (usually accompanied by a meeting with management to provide additional detail and to answer questions that may not have been immediately evident to the original team). At this point, the team members remain available as resources as needed, but the impetus for shifting from the more localized enhancements to the corporate redesign opportunities is now owned by the management team.

CHAPTER 5

Designing Structural Integrity

We trained hard, but it seemed that every time we were beginning to form a team we would be reorganized. We tend to meet every situation by reorganizing and a wonderful method it can be for creating the illusion of progress while producing confusion, inefficiency, and demoralization.

—Gaius Petronius Arbiter, c. 27 to 66 AD,
Author of *Satyricon*

At the toll booth at each end of the Albert Bridge, which spans the Thames in London, is a simple placard: "Notice: Troops Must Break Step When Marching Over This Bridge." The command to "Break Step" (or the American equivalent to "Route Step, March") is a direction to troops to abandon the highly regimented, synchronized cadences suggestive of military parades and, instead, to individualize their movements. Counter to the military's rigorously syncopated activities, "Break Step" is an uncommon order—except when crossing a suspension bridge—a tradition dating back to early 19th-century Britain.

Captain Samuel Brown turned experiments using metal chains to replace the hemp ropes used for ship cables into a series of patents, including one for wrought iron chain links. Using his patented ideas, he built a suspension bridge across the River Tweed, linking England and Scotland. When opened on July 26, 1820, the Union Bridge (so named for having connected the two countries) was—with its 423-foot span between support towers—the longest iron suspension bridge in the world and the first designed to accommodate vehicle traffic.

In fitting acknowledgment of his accomplishment, seated in his carriage, Captain Brown was the first to cross the newly opened bridge, followed by 12 heavily loaded carts, and then by hundreds of spectators who had gathered for the event.[1] The Union Bridge, as acknowledged in an 1826 issue of the *Edinburgh Philosophical Journal*, had proven itself to be "a remarkable combination of strength and lightness."[2] Unfortunately, the measures of "strength and lightness" weren't universally applied in the construction of suspension bridges. The Broughton Suspension Bridge, for example, built in 1825 to span the River Irwell only lasted five years before it collapsed. As the 1831 issue of the *Philosophical Magazine* reported, on April 12, 1831, 74 men marching four abreast from the 60th regiment attempted to cross the Broughton Bridge:

> the men, . . . found that the structure vibrated in unison with [their] measured step . . . as a greater number of them got upon the bridge, the vibration went on increasing . . . They were then alarmed by a loud sound . . . and immediately one of the iron pillars supporting the suspension chains . . . fell towards the bridge [which] immediately fell to the bottom of the river, . . . and from the great inclination thereby given to the roadway, nearly the whole of the soldiers . . . were precipitated into the river.[3]

The ensuing investigation identified that one bolt securing the chains to the masonry had snapped; others were bent and cracked. As reported by the *Manchester Chronicle* a few days after the accident, the bolt had failed owing to the troop's cadence:

> the peculiar manner in which the soldiers marched whilst on the bridge had no slight share in causing the accident . . . The uniform motion naturally gave great agitation to the bridge, the violent effects of which would be most severely felt at the end.[4]

Other suspension bridges—including the Angers Bridge in France that collapsed in 1850, the Wheeling Suspension Bridge in the United States that collapsed in 1854, or the famous swaying, twisting, and ultimate collapse of the Tacoma Narrows Bridge in 1940—succumbed to similar resonance caused by marching or winds—or, stated differently, by a misbalance between lightness and strength. And while other suspension bridges have failed, the Union Bridge—now a "listed building" (a protected heritage site) in both England and Scotland—continues carrying road traffic across the Tweed 200 years after its opening.

The architectural lesson Samuel Brown had learned was revealed in an 1868 lecture by Charles Bender, a civil engineer who, like Brown, had patents for the "improvement of suspension bridges" by "diminish[ing] the side motion caused by the wind."[5] Like Archimedes' epiphany concerning the principle of buoyancy, he explained that

> The invention of the suspension bridge by Samuel Brown sprung from the sight of a spider's web hanging across the path of the inventor, observed in a morning's walk, when his mind was occupied with the idea of bridging the Tweed.[6]

What physicists have since discerned, and Samuel Brown evidently intuited, is that "by better understanding the unique structural properties of spider webs, researchers could apply the information to other areas, such as designing buildings, bridges, and space structures." This conclusion is predicated on the fact that "although the orb web of a spider is a lightweight structure, it seems to be a highly optimized structure."[7] A spider's web—to use the description applied to the Union Bridge—is "a remarkable combination of strength and lightness."

Two kinds of thread are interwoven: radial threads, which are stronger and thicker, radiate out from the center of the web; spiral threads connect the radial threads together. The vertical and horizontal balancing of strength, lightness, and configuration are fashioned to capture quarry while, at the same time, to maximize the web's resilience in resisting forces such as wind. Complementing these factors is the web's versatility. "Spiders can change the number of radial or spiral threads without reducing the strength of the web. This versatility is likely very useful for spiders to adapt the web to various environments."

The attributes of success (strength, lightness, and configuration)—the interlinking and coordination among vertical and horizontal units as epitomized in the design of the Union Bridge (and a spider's web)—also apply to determining successful organizational design for businesses. Organizational effectiveness is dependent primarily on three factors: (1) the coordination and cooperation among functions; (2) optimization as can be achieved through process design, training, and technology; and (3) adaptability and versatility.

A Brief Perspective on Organizational Design

In the opening chapter of his book, *The Structuring of Organization*, a text that has influenced much of contemporary thinking regarding organizational design, Henry Mintzberg, the Cleghorn Professor of Management Studies at McGill University, describes this fundamental nature of organization:

> Every organized human activity—from the making of pots to the placing of a man on the moon—gives rise to two fundamental and opposing requirements: the division of labor into various tasks to be performed and the coordination of these tasks to accomplish the activity. The structure of an organization can be defined simply as the sum total of the ways in which it divides its labor into distinct tasks and then achieves coordination among them.[8]

Given this simple truth, it is not surprising that there is a significant volume of guidance available relating to organizational design; however, often the emphasis of the guidance is on design (arrangement of a company's functional units) rather than on organization (the strategy by which those units will function). In other words, the guidance lacks attention to the need and process for aligning organizational structure with company strategy.

Rather, the majority of popular literature offers a basic model—depicting simple, hierarchical charts of a presumed company's principal functional elements. For instance, a single vertical grouping on the company's proposed organization chart may have "Finance" identified in the uppermost box. Extending downwards are the contributing agencies, for example, accounts payable, accounts receivable, general ledger, financial reporting, and fiscal compliance.

Four variants of this simplified organizational model are most commonly displayed:

- The geographical variant employs columns to represent regions and subregions. The model is proposed for companies with a broad distribution of markets, each subject to unique demands (e.g., different customer bases, different regulations).
- The customer version uses columns to delineate communities of customers. Its structure is intended separately to address each community's specific requirements, expectations, or opportunities.
- The functional option is the most common variant. Using columns assigned to primary business or operating units, its use is suggested for companies with a limited number of products, production processes, markets, or differentiated customer bases.
- Finally, the program variation uses columns to indicate services offered by the company. Like departments in a university or the specialties in a hospital, each column represents a particular service. Sub-elements can range from specific features of the service to communities served, to a listing of attributes (e.g., administration).

These commonly depicted structures, in and of themselves, are not a problem; each of the variants has potential application in a wide span of companies. Rather, the issue is one of lost opportunity: superimposing an organizational structure on a company without careful and deliberate analysis is like buying machinery without knowing if it will work: the organizational structure may or may not support or advance the company's goals, production, or performance.

Before formalizing an organizational structure, companies must consider the implications of such factors as the intended approach to control, the process for decision making, the amount of specialization and training, the division of labor, and the flow of authority.

For instance, implementing any of the four traditional organizational designs just presented is implicitly endorsing and assuming the company's intent to employ much of the early 20th-century managerial philosophies underpinning these structures, principally the theories of Frederick Winslow Taylor and Henri Fayol.

Strongly advocating this hierarchical structure, Frederick Winslow Taylor's two influential texts (*Shop Management* and *The Principles of Scientific Management*) asserted that exclusive functions of management were "rigidly to enforce consistency of work: instituting the 'science' of scientific management, displacing previous rule-of-thumb approximations, selecting and training workers, monitoring performance, and maintaining shop discipline."[9] Henri Fayol's *General and Industrial Administration*, another extremely influential text, echoed Taylor's highly centralized model of control. The first 6 of the 14 management principles Fayol asserted in his text were division of work, authority, discipline, unity of command, unity of direction, and subordination of individual interest.

The lingering effect of this philosophy is the mistaken assumption that the positioning of functional elements on an organization chart is synonymous with the development of a business strategy:

> At least until recently, the underlying assumptions of organizational design have been that organizations require articulated objectives, sharp divisions of labor, clearly defined tasks, well developed hierarchies, and formalized systems of control. In fact, this configuration of elements . . . appears to remain the predominant conception among practitioners in government, mass production, and the consulting profession: to many of them [this set of conditions is] not just one alternative form of structure, it is structure.[10]

As opposed to the formalized structure envisioned as the norm by Taylor and Fayol, modern theories stress the need for purposeful design of the organizational structure, aligning the organization and the organizational systems with the culture, the mission, and the intended modes of conducting business. Among these theories, we have found the work of Henry Mintzberg to be the most useful in providing a practical and pragmatic basis by which to assist in presenting the considerations and components of organizational design that contribute to aligning form with function.

Akin to Stephen Toulmin's methodology for dissecting argument (Chapter 2), Mintzberg reveals and demonstrates the factors and principles controlling the coordination, interactions, and opportunities exhibited in various organizational designs.

Imparting Strength

Understanding Corporate Communities

Mintzberg, who has earned more than a dozen honorary degrees from universities around the world, segregates the organizational structure into a three-part system. The uppermost segment is occupied by the "strategic apex." This level, akin to a company's front office, has as its principal responsibilities the charge to ensure the company achieves its mission while meeting obligations to the agencies that oversee it (e.g., boards of managers and regulatory agencies).

Internal to the company, the strategic apex provides a broad supervisory role—designing the organization, overseeing resource allocation, instituting policy, and administering salary, benefits, and incentives. To the outside world, the group represents the company's voice in the marketplace.

Bridging these internal and external responsibilities, as the unit's title suggests, the strategic apex sets the strategic direction and is central to strategic decisions.

> Strategy formulation . . . involves the interpretation of the environment and the development of consistent patterns in streams of organizational decisions ("strategies") to deal with it. Thus, in managing the boundary conditions of the organization, the [Strategic Apex constitutes the] managers of the formulation of [the company's] strategy.

As Mintzberg goes on to explain about the group's characteristics,

> the strategic apex takes the widest, and as a result the most abstract, perspective of the organization. Work at this level is generally characterized by a minimum of repetition and standardization,

considerable discretion, and relatively long decision-making cycles. Mutual adjustment [cooperation fostered by informal communications] is the favored mechanism for coordination among the managers of the strategic apex itself.[11]

The center section of Mintzberg's three-part organizational structure is jointly occupied by three distinct communities: the technostructure, the middle line, and the support staff. The technostructure is composed of "analysts," people who typically are not involved in the physical work such as production, but, rather, are the architects of the company's processes and programs. They are responsible for designing the way work is done and the procedures and practices used to perform the work. In large part, the analysts are agents of standardization: work study analysts who standardize work processes; planning analysts who standardize outputs; and personnel analysts who standardize skills.

These analysts can be engaged in any of the three sections of the organizational hierarchy, from scheduling production and monitoring how technicians do work, training middle-level managers on company technology, or assisting senior management by designing planning systems such as sophisticated earned value management systems (EVMS) used to track cost and schedule performance. As with personnel in the upper tier (strategic apex), coordination among members of the technostructure is achieved principally through mutual adjustment.

The middle line, the second component in this center section of the corporate structure, includes the entire management chain extending from the strategic apex down to first-line supervisors. Consistent with most expectations for management, the middle line provides the pipeline of direction and information: directions and expectations regarding performance and behavior flow downward; feedback on how well the organization is performing against these expectations flows upward. Succinctly put:

the middle-line manager performs all the managerial roles of the chief executive, but in the context of managing his own unit . . . He must serve as a figurehead for his unit and lead its members;

develop a network of liaison contacts; monitor the environment and his unit's activities and transmit some of the information he receives into his own unit, up the hierarchy, and outside the chain of command; allocate resources within his unit; negotiate with outsiders; initiate strategic change; and handle exceptions and conflicts.[12]

Lastly within this center section is the support staff. Support staff provide the company's administrative and business expertise, for example, general counsel, communications, payroll, and human labor relations.

At the base of the three-part structure is the operating core, the staff who perform the actual work involved in the production of the company's services and products. In general, this community has four primary functions: (1) they coordinate the selection, procurement, and management of the raw materials needed for production; (2) they do the actual work that assembles or creates the final products; (3) they coordinate or perform the marketing and sales of products and services; and (4) they provide the accountability for maintaining the production capabilities (i.e., equipment and facility maintenance, warehousing, inventory control, and property management). Figure 5.1 is a basic depiction of the three-part organizational structure.

With this characterization of the communities comprising a company (a structure readily recognizable as the foundational elements of all companies), the next two factors that need to be ascertained in the process of establishing both strength and versatility of the organizational design are the logic of decision making and the formulation and dissemination of governance. These factors constitute the discriminators

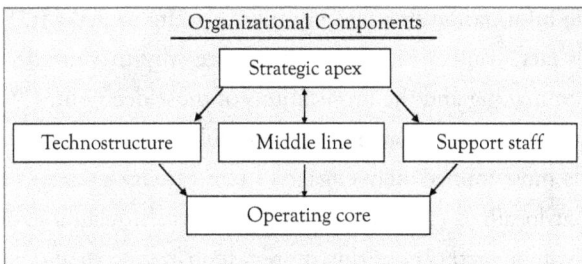

Figure 5.1 *Mintzberg's perception of organization*

and interplay among the segments of Mintzberg's structure, and, as such, represent the bases by which to develop detailed organizational arrangements.

The approaches introduced regarding decision making, flow of authority, and flow of information determine the particulars of organizational design, adding details about the functioning of and integration among the units (i.e., defining supporting programs and interfaces among the three components of Mintzberg's organizational hierarchy). As example, based on the management's intended strategies for conducting work (the approach to decision making, flow of authority, and flow of information), an engineering department might be organized in several different ways: partitioned into its various disciplines (e.g., mechanical, chemical, and civil); maintained within a single, integrated engineering function; distributed among the production lines on a matrixed arrangement; or as outsourced, with services subcontracted as needed.

Authority and Decision Making

As was noted, the authority to make decisions is perhaps the most fundamental component of asserting power within a company. In its most basic form, decision making is either centralized, resident at a single point in the organization, or decentralized (dispersed among several organizations). Although small companies with few products or production lines may work well centralizing decisions with senior management, more complex operations typically require some degree of decentralization of decision making to be effective.

An important factor often overlooked when considering decentralized decision making is that "having the power to make a decision gives one neither the information nor the cognitive capacity to make it."[13] Recognizing this fact, companies need to recognize why they are decentralizing decision making and the implications of those decisions: (1) aligning power with knowledge, placing decision making in the hands of those individuals most immediately engaged in an activity so as to have confidence that localized challenges (production levels, technical, cost, and schedule) will be met; (2) desiring more responsiveness in anticipation of identified global risks (a situation with a potential for reducing company revenues); (3) demonstrating trust in a particular function, manager, or management chain to optimize the role of a particular specialization—an assignment of authority that can also be an effective tool in retaining key personnel; and/or (4) testing and evaluating the capabilities and potential of personnel.

Attention to the complexity of decision making is also a factor in determining the appropriate organizational design. Decision making may be assigned selectively to one or more organizations, or it may be assigned as part of a continuum of decisions. For example, in completing a major project, one department might be given authority to determine the options available for completing the project, but three other departments may, in succession, have authority for determining which option will be implemented, securing the resources and subcontractors needed, and the plan's actual implementation.

Given these considerations, in the case of vertical decentralization, three factors must be considered: (1) What decision powers are to be delegated? (2) How far down the management chain should authority be delegated? (3) What coordination among the levels of delegation is needed and how will it be achieved?

When intending horizontal decentralization, multiple options exist, each with a distinct message and purpose: (1) assigning decision-making authority to an individual, or more particularly to a specific office, establishes the selected function as having the lead in activities involving counterpart organizations; (2) delegating to members of the technostructure signals a plan for the expansion of standardization of the company's processes; (3) in contrast, decision-making authority ceded to the support staff endorses and signals the expectation that protocols, procedures, and governance are going to be tightened; and finally, (4) if the operating core is given decision-making authority, the message is that production is to be maximized, taking precedence over cost, schedules, and (in some instances) safety.

Defining the Governance Framework

As has been noted, authority can be centralized, fully decentralized, or assigned to a specific resident within an organization (i.e., selectively decentralized). Similarly, the form and use of governance can differ markedly depending on the company's operating strategy. In large corporations, the uppermost framework for controlling the business of the company is a document establishing corporate governance policies and practices. Typically, this policy document lays out the fundamental obligations and functioning of the board of directors for overseeing the exercise of corporate powers to ensure the company's business and affairs are effective and ethical (i.e., in keeping with an appropriate standard of care as was discussed in Chapter 1). The requirements stipulated in policies, as discussed in Chapter 2, may also flow down through a series of implementing document levels and document types (e.g., procedures, manuals, and desktop instructions).

While that senior corporate governance document establishes the means for securing coordination among the members of the board, there are four distinct means by which the vertical and horizontal coordination are maintained among the levels below the board of directors. As was mentioned, among the members of the strategic apex and the technostructure, the predominant form of coordination is what Mintzberg refers to as "mutual adjustment." In other words, the relationship among members in each of the two communities is achieved by "the simple process of informal communication."[14] Ironically, while mutual adjustment is the simplest of coordination techniques, it is best reserved for use in complex organizational structures.

Unlike functional components that can be standardized because they are composed of routine, repeating, and fixed tasks and activities, complex (and newly formed) relationships among members of the strategic apex and the technostructure require the flexibility to respond quickly and collectively to changing conditions and expectations. For example, the success and safety of a first-of-a-kind experiment using hazardous materials may depend on the immediate and unscripted coordination among management, scientists, engineers, and safety professionals—all concurrently reacting from their respective perspectives to the evolving circumstances as the experiment progresses, with conversations and impromptu meetings serving as the primary vehicles for communications.

For the remaining functions (middle management, support staff, and operating core), coordination is most commonly achieved through various forms of standardization: standardization of work processes using procedures, policies, and drawings; standardization of outputs by specifying the particular attributes of the product to be delivered; and standardization of skills, achieved through corporate training and other professional development programs.

In developing the role and types of governance that are best aligned with the company's mission and vision, it is also common to emphasize selective decentralization, authorizing a particular organization to develop and implement a rigorous set of controls to which all affected organizations within the company are accountable. For instance, in a company that develops a large number of proposals in response to government-issued solicitations, the integrity of the company's estimating process is critical. Assuring the consistency of methodology and the accuracy, completeness, and currency of cost data submitted by multiple organizations represents the difference among underpricing a proposal, resulting in potential losses if awarded the contract; overpricing a proposal, causing the company to lose out to competitors; and an estimate that accurately reflects the company's advantages in responding to the scope, assumptions, and specifications of the solicitation. Figure 5.2 depicts these interrelated elements that warrant careful attention in the process of constructing the organization.

Maintaining the Alignment

Having established the components of the organizational design does not mean that no further attention to the attributes just discussed is warranted. As circumstances change and strategies evolve, periodic reviews are needed. The basic reason why this periodic and thorough reassessment of organizational design is needed—re-examining the flow of authority,

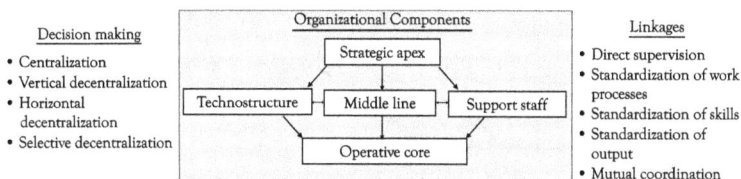

Figure 5.2 The elements of organizational design

the centralization or decentralization of decision making, and the judicious institution of governance—can be illustrated in a single example.

Starbucks, with $29 billion revenue and some 400,000 employees around the world, built its progressive reputation on three elements: (1) positioning "Starbucks as the premier purveyor of the finest coffee in the world,"[15] (2) establishing itself—using the slogan developed by Starbucks' first chief marketing officer—as "the third place," a comfortable environment to relax between home and office,[16] and (3) committing to "direct engagement and the support for the wellbeing of our . . . partners" [Starbucks' term for its employees].[17]

While its reputation for quality coffee has been uninterruptedly sustained since the company's founding in 1971, the company has faltered on its two other defining attributes. These current challenges do not stem from the way in which the elements of the company are arranged; that aspect of organizational design—which is a hybrid of the four basic structural formulations discussed earlier—has remained a successful means of administering the global enterprise. Rather, problems have arisen from a continually expanding distance between the embedded organizational parameters and evolving operational realities, a consequence in large part owing to Starbucks' phenomenal growth (from 425 locations in 1994 to more than 34,000 in 2021) and its relatively recent shift in strategy—concentrating on takeout orders—precipitated by the pandemic.

Once recognized for its progressive thinking (e.g., it was the first company to offer stock options to all employees, including part-time workers), Starbucks' current difficulties are readily understood when examining the thinking underpinning its organizational design. With a structure that currently involves a hierarchy of eight layers of management from the chief executive officer to the baristas, and more than 40 senior executives with policy-setting authority, Starbucks has heavily relied on centralization of decision making at the senior management level. That determination, in turn, tightly limits localized authority and has built reliance on restrictive process controls that recently have collectively instigated a burgeoning drive for unionization along with a broadening challenge to Starbucks' reputation and worker relations.

This centralization of decision making has contributed to supply chain issues and to dissatisfaction among employees who have perceived the company as dismissive of employee-raised issues regarding training, safety, and wages. At the same time, the centralized authority has precluded localized initiatives aimed at enhancing working conditions and community relations. Compounding these factors, exacting governance has damaged worker relations—in particular owing to the continuance of unpopular shift notification practices and the use of a practice known among employees as "clopening," assigning someone to a shift that involves closing a store followed by assignment to a shift that requires opening the same store only a few hours later.[18]

In the language used by Mintzberg, Starbucks has created further difficulty by placing the technostructure in conflict with the operating core. Starbucks' policy sets the expectation that a "partner" should be able to handle the entire process (from taking the order through producing the order, to receiving payment) for 10 customers within the span of 30 minutes.[19] Against the backdrop of this already difficult quota, Starbucks, in keeping with its shifting focus on the takeout market, introduced technology that has created a working situation that effectively prevents employees from achieving this performance expectation.

The introduction of Starbucks' mobile application, "Deep Brew," has had several impacts: it has appreciably increased the volume of orders, creating competition for baristas' attention between mobile and in-store customers; it has accelerated the shift away from the relaxed image of Starbucks as "the third place"; and it has introduced rework and delay in both the production and customer-interaction processes (a consequence of dealing with frequent errors in online orders and with customers aggravated by the fact that the application does not indicate when a requested product or ingredient is unavailable).

As a consequence of these incompatibilities between centralized direction and evolving changes in frontline interactions with customers—precluding local stores from tailoring appropriate accommodating strategies, excluding them from the decision-making process, minimizing authority consigned to local store management, and expecting strict adherence to inviolable governance—"partners" have been rendered less efficient; relationships between workers and customers have been strained; worker satisfaction has plummeted; and the company is no longer held in the high esteem it once merited.

In the simplest of terms, Starbucks is experiencing a growing disconnect between its organizational design and its corporate strategies. To recover, Starbucks must either change the design to meet a new strategy, or it must successfully rebalance the authority, decision making, and governance consistent with the company's current mission: "To inspire and nurture the human spirit—one person, one cup and one neighborhood at a time."[20]

A Reconsideration of Organizational Design Models

Putting the components of Mintzberg's analysis together as a package creates a clear picture of the relationship between an organization's strategy and its structure. In contrast to the basic organizational designs discussed previously that focus on positioning scopes of work relative to one another, a complete appreciation of the relationship between organization and strategy requires analysis of the three factors we have been examining: (1) identifying which part of the organization is the primary link to the company's success or failure; (2) the means by which the organization coordinates activities; and (3) the inclusiveness of the decision-making process. Focusing on these three factors, Mintzberg concluded that the strategy an organization adopts and the extent to which it practices that strategy are reflected in one of five organizational configurations:

Simple structure: The simple structure is most commonly used in relatively new companies and in small corporations, such as a medium-sized office supply firms. There are only one or two top managers, with the remainder of the staff essentially composed of the operating core—shop floor workers. The simplicity of the operation (both scale and complexity) limits the need for middle-level management, support staff, or technostructure; encourages informal communication; and relies on direct supervision of staff for coordination. Centralization of decision making and authority allows the company to respond essentially instantaneously to market changes, disruptions in the supply chain, or the need to restructure processes. As would be expected, as the company grows and the complexity and breadth of work expands, this simple structure is generally replaced by one of the other models.

Machine bureaucracy: Machine bureaucracy places emphasis on the technostructure to design and standardize work processes. Minimal horizontal coordination is needed among the various specializations, but may, depending on the number and complexity of subspecialties, require several levels of management to ensure an appropriate degree of efficiency, standardization, and vertical coordination. As an example, the U.S. Forest Service is one of 15 agencies comprising the U.S. Department of Agriculture. Within the Forest Service System program, there are 18 divisions addressing such specializations as forest management, range management, and management of wild horse and burro territories—each requiring several levels of supervision.

As would be expected given the reliance on standardization of work processes, the machine bureaucracy model works well in stable companies; in contrast, companies that periodically change their strategy would incur the costs and production delays associated with the need to redesign most, if not all, corporate practices and procedures with every change in strategy.

Professional bureaucracy: Professional bureaucracy has an operating core made up of skilled professionals. Designed to provide a balance of governance and autonomy, the model entails a management framework that establishes parameters for the work but then entrusts the performance to the skills and capabilities the professionals bring with them to the job. As skilled professionals, minimal support is required from either the management or a separate technostructure. Rather, the performance of the professionals is principally dependent on the availability of support staff to provide all the necessary administrative and business services. For example, while a high school may be run by a principal and assistant principal, teachers—acting within set parameters associated with classroom behavior and curriculum and supported by both a local and a district staff of administrative and business personnel—have a significant degree of autonomy within their individual classrooms.

Divisionalized form: In what might be considered a collection of machine bureaucracies administered by common management, in this model, the company places emphasis on the middle line, which has responsibility for a number of semiautonomous divisions. Each division works on completing similar tasks, using a commonality of procedures, and with similarly staffed workforces. As such, this organizational design is well suited for companies with a variety of product or service lines, for companies that are required to segregate parts of the company to meet regulatory or legal constraints (as might be the case in which a company has both for-profit and not-for-profit components), and companies that need to minimize potential business risks (for instance, establishing multiple divisions so as to avoid having large shares of the company susceptible to adverse impacts from the same encroaching competition or from the same sources of market volatility).

Adhocracy: In lieu of a typical hierarchical structure, this model has the goal of promoting innovation and maximizing the ability and timeliness of adapting to challenges or opportunities. To accomplish these aims, a segment of the workforce is entrusted with the responsibility for providing appropriate, creative, and innovative leadership of the company, while at the same time minimizing the formality of structure, coordinating activities using mutual adjustment, and selectively decentralizing decision making. In this structure, the technostructure is merged with the operating core and buttressed by a large support staff with the capability, capacity, and flexibility to respond expediently to the dynamic environment.

Although the fluid and organic environment of an adhocracy is often depicted in the media as the idealized business setting, the lack of a defined power structure, the application of selective decentralization, and the independence of key personnel may cause internal friction as the company grows or if it is forced to contract. Consequently, companies that start off using this adhocracy model, over time, tend to shift into one of the other organizational designs (most commonly, into the divisionalized form). Table 5.1 summarizes the attributes of each of the five structural configurations.

Maintaining a Lightness That Complements the Strength

Complementing the strength of the organizational structure is the opportunity to take advantage of the lessons we have been sharing regarding process, training, and technology—opportunities to reduce costs, improve spans

Table 5.1 Attributes of the five organizational configurations

Model Attribute	Simple System	Machine Bureaucracy	Professional Bureaucracy	Divisionalized Form	Adhocracy
Principal advantage	Quick decision making; nimble	Highly efficient; maximizes output	Maximizes use of company expertise	Balances production and risk strategies	Maximizes innovation and adaptability
Primary organizational component	Strategic apex	Technostructure	Operating core	Middle line	Support staff
Principal role of primary organization	Conducts all administrative work	Defines work activities and processes	Provides skilled, standardized work capability	Manages operations	Defines supply, production, and resourcing strategies
Primary form of coordination	Direct supervision	Standardization of work processes	Standardization of skills	Standardization of outputs	Mutual adjustment
Centralization/decision making	Vertical and horizontal centralization	Limited horizontal decentralization	Vertical and horizontal decentralization	Limited vertical decentralization	Maximum use of selective decentralization
Flow of authority	Significant from top	Significant throughout	Insignificant (except in support staff)	Significant throughout	Insignificant or greatly limited
Informal communication flow	Significant	Generally discouraged	Significant for support staff	Limited	Significant throughout
Training required	Minimal	Significant for operating core	Significant	Limited	Minimal
Governance required	Minimal	Significant	Minimal	Required for functional interfaces	Limited

of control, and eliminate duplication of functions while at the same time improving operational efficiency and performance.

For example, let's return to our discussion in Chapter 2 and the problem our original team set out to resolve. The problem addressed by that team was how to improve the process of receipt control and how best to serve the personnel at each of the five company locations. The challenge included coordinating locations with different specializations and operations, different levels of receipt control training, different staffing levels, and different supporting infrastructures (e.g., facilities for receipt, storing, and maintaining procured materials). Figure 5.3 shows the company organization structure (a divisionalized form) as it would have existed at the beginning of the team's assessment. Table 5.2 summarizes the conditions and capabilities at each of the five company locations as previously determined by the team.

By taking advantage of process enhancements, training, and technology, the company could introduce a range of improvements and enhancements, including:

- Reducing the number of locations providing receipt control services
- Automating the process
- Reducing staffing needs

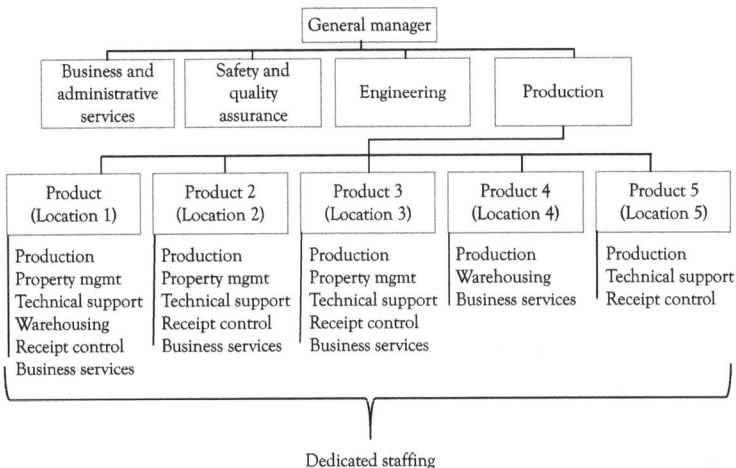

Figure 5.3 Top-level organizational structure

Table 5.2 Data collected by initial process enhancement team

	Location 1	Location 2	Location 3	Location 4	Location 5
Dedicated property management personnel on site	Y	Y	Y	N	N
Access to company property management system	Y	Y	N	N	N
Automated procurement process	Y	N	N	N	N
Technical staff (e.g., engineering) on site	Y	Y	Y	N	Y
Orders and receives sensitive material	N	N	Y	N	Y
Warehouse capability on site	Y	N	N	Y	N
Deliveries to field as well as office	N	N	N	Y	Y
Personnel trained in receipt control	Y	Y	Y	N	Y
Location receives hazardous materials	N	N	N	Y	N
Location relies on corporate capability (e.g., accounts payable)	N	N	N	N	Y
Majority of procurements are for standard off-the-shelf items	Y	Y	N	Y	N

- Improving data management, including linking of property, records, warehousing, and performance management applications
- Maximizing utilization of facilities (e.g., warehouses)
- Reducing the number of organizational interfaces and the associated governance

- Improving the efficiency of operations
- Improving the working relationship among managers, requisitioners, buyers, property managers, project controls professionals, and finance personnel
- Improving safety in the handling and control of hazardous and dangerous materials

The basic mechanisms for achieving these enhancements are summarized in Table 5.3.

As substantive as are those changes, the lessons about organizational models suggest the possibility of an even more significant enhancement—moving from the company's current business strategy to an entirely new organizational model that substantively redefines the breadth of new business and market opportunities and expands the possibility of additional profits and revenue streams.

The consolidations, process improvements, and technology demonstrate that support services (like receipt control) no longer need to reside within or be replicated in each of the product organizations in order to achieve production efficiencies. Enhancements position the company to consolidate these support functions within the existing business and administrative services directorate. In so doing, that directorate, which previously only provided the governance of the support functions, becomes more efficient. Combining the administration and delivery of the services streamlines decision making, internal coordination, and governance; allows the flow of resources among production units as needed; and releases production from all administrative and training responsibilities for the support functions. The revised organizational design made possible through the implementation of the enhancements is shown in Figure 5.4.

The new organizational structure shifts the company from the divisionalized model to a professional bureaucracy, concentrating and maximizing the effectiveness and energies of the company's technical and professional capabilities; these changes can create an environment of innovation within the production lines that can lead to improved processes, increased production, and new product lines. In turn, production capabilities and volumes can be increased owing to the more focused

Table 5.3 Representative enhancements

	Consolidated receipt control		Location 4	Implementing actions taken
	Locations 1 and 2	Locations 3 and 5		
Dedicated property management personnel on site	Y	Y	Y*	*Personnel made available from consolidations moved from Location 2 to 4
Access to company property management system	Y	Y*	Y*	*Enterprise-wide property management application introduced, automating revised processes
Automated procurement process	Y	Y*	Y*	
Technical staff (e.g., engineering) on site	Y	Y	Y*	Personnel made available from consolidations moved from Location 2 to 4
Orders and receives sensitive material	N	N*	Y*	*Sensitive material and hazardous materials received at single warehouse
Warehouse capability on site	Y	N*	Y	*Standard stock items do not require maintaining a warehouse
Deliveries to field as well as office	N	Y	Y	
Personnel trained in receipt control	Y	Y	Y*	*Training on new processes completed at all locations; personnel assume basic QA, safety reviews
Location receives hazardous materials	N	N	Y	
Location relies on corporate capability (e.g., accounts payable)	N	N*	N	*Consolidation of Locations 3 and 5 negates need for corporate support
Majority of orders are for standard off-the-shelf items	Y	N*	Y	*Combined staffing of Locations 3 and 5 allows for expedited receipt control and timely delivery to requisitioners

*Principal organizational changes and how they are implemented

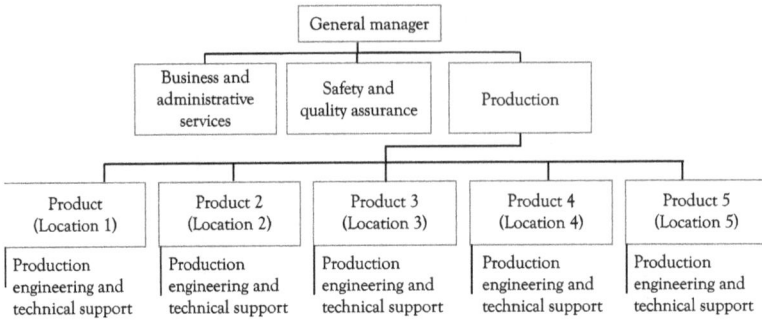

Figure 5.4 The organization transformed into a professional bureaucracy

assignment of the management, the technostructure, and the operating core. Over time, collectively, these enhancements and shifts in business strategy may suggest changes in business lines, marketing strategies, and customer bases.

And, with the continued improvement of performance enhanced through selective decentralization of individual production units, a further metamorphosis may occur. The unleashing of technical personnel (the technostructure) has the possibility of moving the company from a professional bureaucracy to an adhocracy—with all the accompanying benefits for the company's long-term performance and sustainability.

The bottom-line value to companies from conducting a comprehensive and disciplined approach to organizational design is evident: alignment of organizational design and strategy—complemented by the enhancements delivered by process improvements, training, and technology—can (in the words used to describe the Union Bridge) assist in transforming a company into a business that is "a remarkable combination of strength and lightness."

CHAPTER 6

Acting Strategically

However beautiful the strategy,
you should occasionally look at the results.

—Winston Churchill

Originally the bookkeeper for the company, in 1856, Joseph Schlitz purchased a small local brewery that was to become the Schlitz Brewing Company. While in the process of steadily growing the business, Mr. Schlitz's vision of a beer empire got an unanticipated jumpstart when the Chicago Fire of 1871 wiped out a majority of the local competition. Seizing the opportunity, Schlitz's strategy involved not only expanding his production, but, rather, redefining the industry.

The company's modest beginnings were replaced by a multifacility complex complemented by a range of innovations: Schlitz enhanced the beer's quality by bringing the first pure culture yeast strain to the United States; the company partnered in establishing the Union Refrigerator Transit Company, creating a cost-effective refrigerated freight line; and it introduced brown bottles to protect the beer from sunlight during shipping.

By 1902, Schlitz was producing in excess of one million barrels per year. By the 1960s, its capacity reached five million barrels. Nevertheless, by the 1970s, Schlitz's major competitors (Anheuser Busch, Miller, and Pabst) had surpassed it in production volumes.

Something had to be done! The CEO at the time, Robert Uihlein (a descendent of Joseph Schlitz), had a strategy for rescuing the "beer that made Milwaukee famous." Unfortunately, Uihlein's strategy took little heed of the company's traditions and customer base, totally dismissing the product's reputation as "the most carefully brewed beer in the world." Rather, Uihlein was about to unleash what has been deemed "The Schlitz

Mistake," a series of strategic miscalculations that forever tarnished the product, insulted the customer base, and then drove them away.

Driven by profit goals and a commitment to regain production dominance in the industry, Uihlein introduced his strategy through a cascading series of changes that progressively made Schlitz beer and the company less palatable. As a first step, to increase throughput, Schlitz speeded up the fermentation process; the process, initially touted as "Accelerated Batch Fermentation" by the company, reduced brewing cycle time from 25 to 21 days, and then from 21 to 15 days—less than half the time allotted by competitors. When challenged by competitors "claiming that its ABF brewing method meant it was selling 'green,' or too-young beer," Schlitz sought to mask its activities by changing the meaning of its ABF designation from "accelerated batch fermentation" to "accurate balanced fermentation."[1]

Having supposedly gotten away with the initial changes in brewing, the next logical means of increasing profits—or so Uihlein thought—was by using cheaper ingredients: replacing fresh hops with dried hops pellets and reducing reliance on barley by adding corn syrup.

But these changes had unanticipated consequences. Because it aged the beer for less time, Schlitz was forced to add silica gel to prevent a hazy substance from forming when the beer was chilled. Seeking to disguise the chemical's use from the public and the U.S. Food and Drug Administration, Schlitz then switched to a different chemical that could be filtered out of the final product, negating the need to list it on the labels as an ingredient. However, this attempted deception created a new problem: A reaction to the new chemical caused protein to settle out. "At its best this protein looked like tiny white flakes floating in the beer and at its worst it looked like mucus, or 'snot,' as one observer bluntly called it."[2]

For months Schlitz kept quiet about the problem, with Uihlein arguing that the haze was not actually physically harmful to drinkers, and in any case not much of the beer would be kept at temperatures at which the haze would form. However, drinkers did complain, sales began to drop, and Schlitz had to make a secret recall of 10 million bottles of beer, costing it $1.4 million.[3]

With a looming market crisis, Schlitz decided it needed a powerful advertising campaign to recapture its customers—inadvertently triggering another near fatal blow to the company.

To stem its declining sales and improve its spiraling reputation, the company hired an ad agency, Leo Burnett & Co., to create four television spots. Unfortunately, like the changes to the production process, the ad campaign, dubbed by the media as the "Drink Schlitz or I'll kill you" campaign, didn't appear amusing as intended, but, rather, was seen as threatening. The result was further declines in sales.[4]

Commercials featured actors offering ostensibly menacing responses to anyone suggesting a switch to a brand other than Schlitz. In one commercial, offering an alternative beer elicits this response: "I'm gonna play Picasso and put you on the canvas!" In another commercial, a mountain-man accompanied by a cougar is asked if he would like to try a different beer. The cougar growls loudly, the mountain-man's axe is highlighted, and then the man looks at the cougar and says: "Say hello to your lunch." Disenchanted customers saw the campaign as one more reason to break faith with the company that had now strayed too far in both product quality and demeanor.

As one writer noted:

> The ads only lasted ten weeks before being pulled, and Schlitz fired the marketing team responsible. But it was too late. Schlitz had sealed its fate . . . Their failure during such a critical time for the brand proved to be detrimental to its already-crumbling reputation.[5]

Yet Uihlein had one last bad decision to impose on the Schlitz Brewing Company. In 1981, Schlitz attempted to reduce production costs by forcing concessions on its workforce. The workers went on strike, contract negotiations dragged on, and then negotiations collapsed. The decision soon thereafter was reached by the board of directors to close the Milwaukee plant, which, in 1982, was sold to the Stroh Brewing Company.

While one member of the Schlitz family had turned a strategy and vision into a major American enterprise that endured for more than a century, it only took one descendent with an ill-framed strategy and a larcenous perspective a few short years to cause the company's absolute demise.

A major lesson taught by the rise and fall of the Schlitz Brewing Company is that strategy needs to start by establishing the basis for the overarching objectives that will drive the vision of the company, but that the vision must be clear, rational, achievable, and in the best interests of the company. Ensuring clarity of vision takes investment in time, resources, and infrastructure to ensure the tools and capability necessary to achieve the strategic vision are in place.

A strategy well defined and well thought out, as Joseph Schlitz aptly demonstrated, can create or strengthen a business model and provide the sustainability through all sorts of changes and disruptions in the industry. A poorly defined strategy diminished by a weak implementation logic, as Robert Uihlein tragically demonstrated, can have an equally substantial—though catastrophic—result.

As these two diametrically opposite strategic visions at the Schlitz Brewing Company attest, it's best to start by taking a moment of reflection, a basic assessment of the company's status, the resources and capabilities available to achieve a new or modified vision, and (as the 60th regiment learned when crossing the Broughton Bridge) a full and disciplined measure of how solid a foundation your company is on before you march your company, its future, and its reputation in a new direction.

A common mistake accompanies those individuals and companies that allow their enthusiasm to propel them immediately into implementing a new strategy. There is a certain allure with getting into motion—jumping to questions about how to proceed: How do we fix this problem, how do we position ourselves for future growth, how do we want to respond to this market disruption, or how do we proceed with this opportunity that will disrupt the entire industry?

Clearly, these are all good questions, and, in time, need to be addressed. But the caution might have been best expressed by Benjamin Franklin when he offered a general caution about prematurely speeding ahead on initiatives: "Don't confuse motion with action!" Getting the right strategy in place, and the right means by which to deliver it, might more appropriately begin with two predicates: (1) Who is going to design and be the force behind the strategy and (2) what does the strategy seek to accomplish?

It is a sequence that, consistent with standard project management principles, suggests that you design a program first by understanding the scope and then the agencies responsible for its delivery. Even a casual reflection on the saga of the Schlitz Brewing Company makes evident the appreciable significance of who's leading the charge and where that charge is leading.

Who's in Charge

Strategic thinking, in general, focuses on finding and developing opportunities that create value by engaging in transparent and creative dialogue among those individuals responsible for defining the company's direction. Good strategic thinking, in particular, focuses on potential opportunities that create value and are free to challenge the existing assumptions and direction of the organization. It is in these evaluations and challenges that the company gains understanding of the attributes of and the contributors to the existing business model, as well as adds to the perspective by which to gage the adequacy of conventional and prevailing thinking about the processes and procedures.

Yet, it needs to be recognized that it can be difficult to think strategically, particularly when that thinking promotes new ideas that might be in direct opposition to what is currently being done. As we have noted in several instances throughout this text, it is critical to push ahead with transparent discussions that use a disciplined methodology to translate vision into well-considered policies, and then to convert those policies into practices, governance, organizational design, and technology decisions.

In so doing, the strategic thinkers in the company need to examine the given situation, searching for the alternatives, identifying operational relationships, but—perhaps most importantly—always challenging the underpinning assumptions. And, at the same time, in defining a new or modified strategy, they must resist the urge to let any single decision drive the determination of strategic initiatives. Rather, there is a need to maintain a broadened perspective that seeks clarity out of complex and seemingly disconnected details. It is a challenge, like the consolidation and standardization of receipt control that the team tackled in Chapter 2, wherein multiple factors (including constraints, technology, and resources) must be synchronized.

However, at the same time, a company must recognize that strategic redefinitions do not necessarily occur spontaneously. Typically, a strategic agent of change can recognize when things are on the precipice of change and is inspired by a recognition of elements in conflict—for example, why is production not meeting expectations, why is market share lower than anticipated, and why are products experiencing a higher than reasonable error rate? This recognition provides the foundation and impetus for defining the strategy: getting to the root of the problem, understanding constraints and interfaces, and, ultimately, shaping and articulating a reasoned path forward predicated on specific and compelling arguments.

However, relying on a change agent to define a path forward may not be synonymous with authorizing that individual or team to move forward with its implementation. As we discussed when examining organizational design in Chapter 5, the authorization of policies and strategies—along with the associated direction and governance—is jurisdictionally reserved for senior management.

Relinquishing control of strategy can become a recipe for chaos. Although it may be healthy for employees generally to have a questioning attitude, changes in strategy need to be seen from the appropriate vantage points if the company is to maintain a level of stability while introducing change. In contrast, if multiple forces are concurrently changing the way things work and how the pieces of the company practices and policies fit together, internal disruptions may become more damaging than externally generated challenges.

As example, one might consider the reactions to the Global Pandemic of 2020. What the pandemic made evident was that change was needed, but not all changes were part of crisply thought-out and executed long-term strategies. What the pandemic identified was whether or not companies were nimble enough to respond to a broad range of unanticipated conditions. Could companies redirect their resources in order to ensure that the company remained solvent and relevant? In other words, did the company have a sustainable business model?

In the period of the pandemic, literally every company was operating in a previously unknown business environment and became subject to external controls and influences over which they had minimal—if any—control.

While a good number of companies suffered financially, and many didn't survive, others brought about some of the most creative industrial change and industry disruption in decades. In so doing, the existing business models had to contend with—among other factors—massive rethinking of cost projection escalations, supply chain methodology, organizational standards, division of labor, and shifting markets to name a few. Those companies that managed to survive (and those that flourished) had to entrust their fates to the individuals who, as we have been describing, took measure of the situation, redefined the modes of doing business, identified the markets (sometimes totally different than those before the pandemic), and then orchestrated the implementation. What they were doing was, in fact, bridging the boundaries between the "who" of the strategic exercise and the "what" that the strategy was seeking to accomplish.

So, What's the Plan

Knowing where you are headed, how to know when you've arrived, and what things are intended to look like when you get there are the three questions that dominate attention once those leaders of your strategic realignment have been authorized to develop comprehensive plans. These plans constitute the foundational road map that sets the pace; lays out the tasks; and defines contributing elements like cost, schedule, risks, and the specific targets of optimization (process enhancement, personnel development, technology additions, adjustments in governance, and realignment of organizational redesign).

In this context and expanding on aspects of strategy evidenced in our discussion of Joseph Schlitz, we might consider how one of his contemporaries, Henry Ford, successfully defended his vision against a substantive challenge. By late 1913, even before the moving assembly lines for which he was famous had been fully implemented throughout the shop, labor turnover at the Ford Motor Company "was a whopping

380 percent. People quit so often that in order to expand the labor force by 100 men, the company had to hire 963."[6] The issue was, as his production supervisors reported, people were intensely bored by assembly line work and were leaving for other jobs in the region with equivalent salaries.

In terms of the Fogg Behavior Model we discussed in Chapter 4, to maintain a stable workforce and achieve the production capabilities he envisioned, Ford needed to re-establish an appropriate balance among ability, motivation, and triggers. Workers were fully qualified and capable, but motivation had plummeted owing to the repetitive nature of work that accompanied assembly line production. Recognizing this fact, Henry Ford instituted an extraordinary set of actions.

On January 7, 1914, a banner across the full length of page 1 above the *Detroit Times*' masthead exclaimed: "Henry Ford's Answer to Hard Times Bogey Is Gift to Millions of Men." The Column One headline explained the revelation: "FORD MOTOR WORKERS GET $10,000,000." In a mix of initial caps and all caps, the subhead summarized the elements of the revolutionary changes underway: "Profit-Sharing Plan Announced By Giant Concern Will Put Half of Earnings into Pockets of Employees; 22,000 MEN WILL REAP BENEFIT OF SCHEME; Hour Clipped From Work Day and 5,000 Will Be Added to Factory Force."[7]

The magnitude of Ford's actions was aptly captured in the article's first paragraph: "An epoch in the world's industrial history was marked in Detroit Monday, and a note struck in the hymn of humanity's progress that will echo throughout the civilized nations of the earth."[8]

As the article went on to describe, Ford had not only immediately raised the average salary from $2.34 per day to a minimum of $5.00 per day or higher based on workers' assignments; he had reduced the average work schedule from 9 to 8 hours a day. Moreover, he instituted a policy that established a new level of worker job security:

No man will be discharged if we can help it except for unfaithfulness or inefficiency. No foreman in the Ford company has the power to discharge a man, He may send him out of his department if they do not make good. The man is then sent to our clearing house covering all the departments and is again repeatedly tried in other work until we find the job he is suited for, provided he is honestly trying to render good service.[9]

This counterbalancing set of motivational factors, coupled with the use of biweekly paychecks and job security as continually evident triggers, immediately changed the fortunes of the Ford Motor Company.

Not surprisingly, these radical steps were quickly demonized by his competitors and by the media. Representative of the response, a *Wall Street Journal* editorial asserted that

To double the minimum wage, without regard to length of service, is to apply Biblical or spiritual principles where they do not belong . . . [Ford has] in his social endeavor committed blunders, if not crimes. They may return to plague him and the industry he represents, as well as organized society.[10]

Nevertheless, the results were as Ford intended. With workers well compensated and now perceived by Ford as "partners" in his enterprise, labor turnover fell the following year from 380 to 16 percent. The reduced working hours allowed Ford to add a third shift, the additional 5,000 positions immediately filled by people attracted to Michigan by the prospect of high-paying, secure jobs.

But, perhaps most important, the changes allowed Ford to fulfill his vision. Quoting a representative of the Ford Motor Company, the *Detroit Times* article concluded with this commitment: "The public need have no fear that this action of ours will result in any increase in prices of our products. On the contrary we hope to keep up our past record of reducing prices each year." True to that vision, by 1919, a Ford Model T that had sold for $800 in 1910 now cost the American consumer only $350.

The lesson that Henry Ford's disruptive policies teach is that a single overarching strategy is often not sufficient. As with the innovations that Joseph Schlitz introduced, the major corporate strategies need to be re-enforced and implemented through well-aligned subtier strategies that bring all forces and programs into line with the global objectives.

Returning now to our current business environment, in comparison to the workforce changes consequent to Ford's actions, the Covid-19 global pandemic has had a much more profound effect. It redefined the nature and attitudes of the principal resource of essentially all businesses: The human resource. Covid-19, in comparison to focused changes on compensation and the work environment influenced by Ford, did not disrupt a particular industry; rather, it permanently disrupted the fundamental principles of business. Along with changes in social habits, massive shifts occurred in markets (e.g., exercise equipment and entertainment products) and in the delivery of products and services (from groceries to medical services). However, more pervasive was the shift in how and where work was performed.

The protracted period of dealing with wave after wave of Covid-19 restrictions caused entire generations to rethink what was important to them. The lengthy reliance on remote work and virtual technology led to a recognition among a large segment of the working population that lifestyle rather than work, job title, or (in many cases) salary was the dominant force in their lives. At the same time, industries—whether voluntarily or in recognition of the new worker reality—began reconsidering fundamental business practices, such as the needs for large, commercially leased office space.

Like Henry Ford, business leaders were forced to look at employment opportunities from a new perspective. While just a few years earlier it was considered progressive to offer employees amenities like daycare and workout centers, the new norm to which industries were pressured to respond became a workforce that may minimally—if at all—be seen working at the company's offices. Relatively overnight, the socioeconomic landscape was reshaped, allowing, for instance, a remote worker to live in a small town in Idaho while working for a major conglomerate in Silicon Valley, CA.

Given the high probability that disruptions (perhaps even some on the scale caused by Covid-19) will continue to occur, business leaders need to know how to react to the challenges, reassess how they manage work, how to reconfigure their companies, and how to reinvent their activities when circumstances warrant.

The first step in this preparation is to optimize the organizational alignment to ensure that there are clear lines of communication accompanied by a governance structure that not only meets the company's needs but also acknowledges the employees' expectations. This balancing requires leaders who can recognize the strategic changes necessary to keep up or (as Henry Ford did) stay ahead of the changes—in markets, personnel management, technology, and working environments—to keep their businesses stable and moving forward. Said differently, it is now a leader's responsibility to create a culture of collaboration and teamwork, built on the foundations of trust, communication, and a governance structure that promotes a sense that employees are (as Ford termed them) "partners" in the success of the enterprise.

This successful "culture of collaboration and teamwork" that fosters development and delivery of effective strategies, is, as should be apparent, a direct consequence of the practices and principles we have been advocating throughout this text. A few of these components with which you are now familiar—organizational alignment, strategic alignment, and effective process design—are worthy of specific attention.

Organizational Alignment

In a postpandemic posture, it is important to ensure that you have the best possible organizational alignment to allow your company to sustain itself and to thrive under a new working environment. Organizational alignment (the outcome of effective strategies addressed in Chapter 5) creates a synergy between the company's vision of success and the individual contributors who ensure results of the business operations are executed.

Organizational alignment, in particular, allows broad participation in initiatives beyond employees' daily activities—contributing to consistency, local ownership, and commitment. By aligning the organizational structure with strategy, it focuses attention on workflow, expectations, and the identification of efficiencies and process improvements.

When executed through structured planning, clear communication of process, and mindful execution of management, organizational alignment is a powerful tool for management and workforce alike. Not only is the collaboration motivating for those immediately involved in an initiative; but using well-positioned, well-respected personnel, as we have stated, provides a vehicle for spreading the efforts, initiatives, and enthusiasm throughout the company.

As might be expected, the lack of organizational alignment has precisely the opposite effect. Misdirected or competing strategies result in rework, lost revenue, and misalignment of resource commitments. Moreover, it is a ready pathway for personnel to lose confidence in the company leadership.

When this occurs, high-performing individuals may step in to try to rescue their respective organizations, creating further divisions among the programs and even less productive, less committed operations. As we saw in our earlier discussion of Mintzberg's characterization of organizations, balance needs to be struck between the latitude for innovation provided to organizations and the control exerted through corporate governance.

Key in achieving this balance are two factors: First is establishing individual and team goals that can be directly correlated with the overarching corporate strategic initiatives; second is active management engagement in monitoring the success and progress of organizational objectives—ensuring they remain on track to produce the intended results, providing both corrections and recognition as appropriate.

Strategic Alignment

Strategies require both vertical and horizontal alignment. Although there is often a single overarching strategy for the company, as suggested by the discussions of the work of Joseph Schlitz and Henry Ford, there are, potentially, strategies at every level of the company. At these more localized levels, strategies—establishing the framework for how work is to be achieved—align vertically with the goals associated with delivering on the organization's mission, vision, and values. Horizontal alignment ensures the compatibility and coordination among strategies.

Well-aligned goals not only increase probability of success, but, at the operational level, also support effective assignment of resources, effective prioritization of work, and clearer definition of the rates and degrees of progress toward achieving objectives. Accordingly, when establishing strategies, company leaders need to ensure strategies in one part of the organization are not inadvertently and inappropriately impacting the ability to achieve strategies in another part of the organization.

Building Strategy From Process

As we have stressed in this text, effective and efficient business processes are a foundation of any successful business. In an ever-changing work environment, routine process improvement provides continual alignment between how work is to be done and the environment in which the work is done. For instance, were one or more of the corporate locations in our receipt control exercise to shift to teleworking or were to dispense with warehousing in favor of just-in-time procurements, the associated changes in constraints and operating strategy would necessitate an entire restructuring of the process that the team had implemented.

Taking a step further back and looking at all processes and their interfaces provides an opportunity to redefine operational discipline, encourage employees to analyze the current state of the business plan, and open a discussion on improvement and optimization throughout the corporation. That opportunity for improvement or optimization is also the opening for establishing performance measurements and metrics.

At its most fundamental level, the use of performance monitoring is to maintain the alignment between performance and expectations and to allow the timely consideration of course corrections if the facts indicate. However, done correctly as a collaborative exercise, introducing this running dialogue between management and employees further solidifies a teamed approach, creating a bond focused on improving company performance, acknowledging successes, and forging a shared mission and vision.

Building Deconstructed Objectives

Deconstructing standards is a term commonly used in education to refer to the practice of establishing learning objectives and incorporating information into lesson plans. As we have explained in our discussions of process enhancement, the common practice for evaluating and improving processes is through development of flow diagrams detailing the sequential steps involved in completing the activity. However, when the effort shifts from a focus on optimization to implementation of an entirely new strategy, a different approach may prove equally, if not more, effective.

Building deconstructed objectives works the concept of process flow in reverse—first setting out the end objective or goal as the target and then working through the process to isolate just those incremental activities necessary to achieve the objective. As a result, the process minimizes or eliminates attention and efforts expended on accommodating current process limitations, constraints, and interfaces that may no longer apply.

In so doing, deconstruction is designed to create a new process rather than fix an old one. As opposed to the typical flow analysis which might only minimize weaknesses and optimize certain components in the process, deconstruction emphasizes total rethinking of the process. And, depending on the magnitude in difference between the original strategy according to which the process was originally formulated and the new strategy—the degree of difference in the targets—deconstruction can yield, as appropriate, either an optimized process or a brand new one.

Once the process has been redefined, organizational associations and a timeline can be created for each action, offering further insights into potential improvements. In addition to the benefits in performance, utilizing the deconstruction method gives process owners a greater perspective and appreciation of how and in what way they contribute to the company's bottom line.

How Can You Help Your Management Team Think Strategically?

Underlying the success in identifying and delivering strategies is the critical thinking applied to solving complex problems and creating achievable plans for the future. In particular, this strategic thinking is composed of four critical components complemented by four approaches to building strategic awareness.

Critical Components of Strategic Thinking

1. *Analytical review*: To develop long- and short-range strategic goals and objectives, it is important to evaluate the current standings of the

company relative to industry competitors. To do this, first identify those data sources that provide points of comparison; these points of reference can range from financial statements and key performance indicators (KPIs) to market conditions, to emerging business trends, and examination of internal resource allocations.

2. *Communication*: Putting a strategy in place for the company requires solid communication skills. The ability to communicate complex ideas, collaborate with internal and external stakeholders, build consensus, and ensure everyone is aligned and working toward shared goals are all central to strategic thinking. Having a communication plan that addresses multiple methods of sharing information with each of the various audiences (e.g., stockholders, employees, and corporate boards) and ensuring that there is alignment with the goals and objectives will enhance the success of implementation. In some instances, bringing in external communication expertise can prove helpful in providing a more objective analysis and better perspective on what messages need to be delivered.

3. *Problem solving*: Implementing a strategy that addresses the central challenges faced within the company requires that everyone first understand the problems at hand and their potential solutions. Issues such as missed financial targets, inefficient processes and procedures, and/or acknowledgment of an emerging competitor all require that the situation be clearly defined and a path to corrective planning and execution be developed.

4. *Planning and management*: Effective strategic implementation relies on disciplined decision making and execution. Once data has been analyzed, the situation is understood by all decision-making parties and a path forward has been clearly identified, it takes strong management and implementation skills to pull everything together into an integrated set of actions and initiatives. Analytical techniques—such as the Toulmin model discussed in Chapter 2—should be used to ensure suitable attention is paid to the underlying assumptions associated with the corporate decisions. Tools like earned value management systems should be employed in the delivery process.

Building Strategic Awareness

1. *Ask relevant questions*: One of the easiest and most effective methods to enhancing your situational awareness is to ask strategically oriented questions—questions about the current strategies, long-term sustainability, emerging markets, and so on. Asking the questions from an array of sources is best suited to getting multiple perspectives—amplifying likelihood of identifying weaknesses and opportunities, as well as defining how most effectively to leverage past and present information and situations in the process of formulating a strategic path forward.

2. *Listen and engage mindfully*: It is easy to get focused on a narrow process, issue, and/or area of responsibility, but it is critical to know and understand the interdependent connections and impacts changes will have. For instance, do not assume the company has adequate processes and/or resources in place to support a strategic initiative; overcommitting can have detrimental effects on performance, company reputation, and employee morale. Instead, gather as much information as possible to use when developing a strategy. Evaluate the data available, make departmental and industry comparisons, and interview stakeholders, clients, and process owners to ensure that everyone is working to the same understanding and expectation. And then make certain capability is commensurate with the challenge.

3. *Consider opposing ideas*: As a follow-on to the previous consideration, be highly self-critical. Utilize critical thinking and an open platform to question your assumptions and strategic goals. When possible, use people other than those individuals who contributed to the decisions to reassess the impacts, challenges, weaknesses of your strategic roadmap, and to gage the probability of achieving a successful implementation of your strategy.

4. *Seek outside resources*: Strategic thinking is limited by your environmental exposure and should not be confused with routine support activities and operational decision making. Not everyone thinks strategically, and it is critical to inform yourself about what strategic trends are being introduced and what fundamental strategic methods are best applied. Don't limit your sources of support; be open to engaging resources within and external to the company.

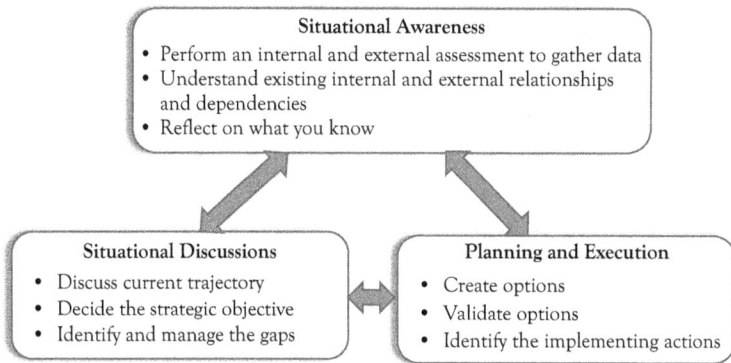

Figure 6.1 The basics of strategy development and delivery

Many businesses inevitably grow complacent when things stay the same for too long. When something finally comes along that disrupts or redefines an industry, the incumbents that do survive almost always give up ground to competitors who have routinely pursued improvements; have maintained alignment among organizational design, governance, and strategy; and have remained diligent in the monitoring of performance, market standing, and industry trends.

Irrespective of your business type or size, if your goals and objectives are aligned with your strategic initiatives, and you are managing and adjusting your resources and trajectory, you have the foundations of a sustainable business model (Figure 6.1).[11] As Sun Tzu noted some 2,500 years ago in the *Art of War* and remains a prudent message for all forms of competition—including business: "Strategy without tactics is the slowest route to victory. Tactics without Strategy is the noise before defeat."

The bottom line: *Invest in your business through strategy and it will offer great rewards.*

CHAPTER 7

Conclusion

Even if you're on the right track, you'll get run over if you just sit there.
—Will Rogers

We thought it fitting since we began this manuscript with Archimedes' famous quotation ("Give me a place to stand, and I shall move the earth") to return in these final pages to the theme of standing on the verge of a great endeavor. And, although not rivaling the magnitude of Archimedes' efforts, in contemporary life what is a more common experience—and more apt metaphor for individual challenge—than a golfer standing in the tee box readying to accept the challenge of the course ahead?

The golf challenge as we know it today began in eastern Scotland as a game of hitting pebbles over sand dunes. Banned in mid-15th century by James II because the game distracted men from military service, it was reinstated early in the 16th century by James IV. Over the next century or so, the game increased in popularity; golf leagues were formed (the first being the Gentlemen Golfers of Leith, 1744); and formal rules of play were enshrined.

With construction of the 18-hole course at St. Andrews, Scotland, in 1764, a new standard of play was established. Further recognition came to St. Andrews in 1834 when King William declared the St. Andrews golf club was heretofore to be known as the "Royal and Ancient Golf Club of St. Andrews" (today referred to simply as the "R&A").

As St. Andrews flourished, a west coast golf club at Prestwick was actively seeking recognition for its golf course and for a local golfer, Tom Morris, whom they believed to be the best in Britain. Recognizing an opportunity to showcase Prestwick, Major James Ogilvy Fairlie, a joint founder of the Prestwick Golf Club and architect of the first ever competition, the 1857 Grand National Golf Club Tournament, proposed a country-wide competition. With plans laid, Prestwick issued a decree to clubs across Britain that "known & respectable Cadies" were welcome to enter this first-of-a-kind tournament.[1]

At noon on October 17, 1860, eight golfers gathered at the 12-hole golf course in Prestwick; rules were read and pairings set. After three rounds, Willie Park (from a rival course just east of Edinburgh) had won; Tom Morris finished second. With allusion to the American Revolution, the local newspaper, the *Ayrshire Advertiser*, voiced the region's disappointment:

> the most veteran frequenters of the Links will admit that in all their experience of Morris, they never saw him come to grief so often, because it is well known that the battle of Bunker's Hill is an engagement which he has very seldom to fight.[2]

For just over a hundred years thereafter, the Open (known previously as the British Open and the Open Championship) has remained one of the four most prestigious tournaments alongside the Masters, the U.S. Open, and the PGA Championship. Yet, among the memorable performances at the Open, there are two the R&A remembers with little fondness.

In 1965, Walter Danecki, a postal worker from Milwaukee, Wisconsin, submitted an entry form to the Open. Unwilling and unable to qualify for American tournaments, he identified himself on the form as "professional." As he reasoned, he was a professional because "it's the money [he was] after." Scoring 108 in the first round followed by 113 in the second round, he was out of the tournament and out of the money. Asked afterward why he didn't just leave the competition after the disappointing first round, he responded that "Nobody likes a quitter."[3] While his rounds set a record as the worst score in Open history, the record was short-lived.

The 1976 (105th) Open started with a field of 155 golfers. Johnny Miller would win his first Open championship, but the newspaper headlines were largely focused on a 19-year-old phenom from Spain, Steve Ballesteros, who tied for second with Jack Nicholas, and on Maurice Flitcroft, a 46-year-old shipyard crane operator from Barrow-in-Furness, England, who, until two years earlier, had never held a golf club. Without a handicap or documentation certifying his status, Flitcroft couldn't qualify as an amateur. So, as Danecki had done, he checked "professional" on his entry form and left blank any questions he couldn't answer. Nonetheless, the R&A awarded him a slot.

In the qualifying round on July 2, 1976, having never before even been on an 18-hole course, Flitcroft, with a set of mail-order clubs, put in a most memorable performance. His opening technique, as described by his partner, immediately caught the attention of the crowd, the media, and the R&A: "After gripping the club as if he was intent on murdering someone, Flitcroft hoisted [his golf club] straight up, came down vertically, and the ball travelled precisely four feet."[4] The rules at the time, unfortunately for the R&A, precluded stopping his play which—as described by one witness—was "a blizzard of double and triple bogeys ruined by a solitary par."[5]

On the front nine, Flitcroft managed a 61, only slightly bettered by a 60 on the back nine. Interestingly, having eclipsed Danecki's course record, his 121 (49 over par) might actually have been understated: Flitcroft's caddy lost count on Hole 7, entering a "12" followed by a question mark on the score card.

In response, after 1976, the R&A changed the entry rules, restricting entry to accomplished golfers whose finishes on the professional circuit gave them "exemptions" and to a limited number of amateurs who qualified based on performance in regional tournaments. Because Flitcroft had entered the 1976 Open as a professional, he now couldn't join a golf club as an amateur; nor could he achieve a "1" handicap needed for professional certification by the Professional Golfers' Association (PGA).

To the R&A's chagrin, changing entry requirements did not mean they had seen the last of Maurice Flitcroft. In 1978, he regained entry into the Open posing as American professional golfer, Gene Paceki ("paycheck"); recognized after the first few holes, he was removed from the course. Following a series of failed entry attempts, in the 1983 Open, Flitcroft resurfaced as Gerald Hoppy, a golfer from Switzerland. Able to complete nine holes before being unmasked, Flitcroft in his Hoppy persona was on course to break his 1976 record—having already reached a score of 63.

Yet Flitcroft was to show up one last time in 1990, this time as American professional, James Beau Jolley (as in Beaujolais). In this outing, he had a double bogey on the first hole, a bogey on the second hole, and was on the third fairway when "he was interrupted by an R&A golf buggy that screeched to a halt in front of him" and ended his play.[6] Exasperated, thereafter the R&A resorted to use of a handwriting analyst to screen signatures on entry forms, ending Flitcroft's streak as "the phantom of the Open."[7]

Although Maurice Flitcroft achieved a modicum of notoriety and received short-lived press coverage (mostly unflattering), his real desire to be recognized as an accomplished golfer was never to be. The simple reason is that he relied exclusively on strategy, a strategy, in this case, that was not buttressed by any of the components essential for success: process efficiency, training, technology, and understanding of underpinning attributes of the culture.

Archimedes' accomplishments, in contrast, were derived from exhaustive study and observation, the design and development of the necessary tools and machinery, and a complete understanding and appreciation of the science he was readying to apply. Flitcroft, in comparison, had little preparation.

Having relied exclusively on a few golf texts, limited practice, poor quality equipment, and his ambition, Flitcroft all but disregarded the effort needed to achieve a level of performance commensurate with his goals. Relying on strategy, he dispensed with understanding, appreciating, and mastering the techniques, tools, and science of the sport. Rather, having been mesmerized by the thought of playing alongside the likes of Jack Nicholas, Flitcroft had maneuvered into, rather than earned, his place in the 1976 Open qualifiers.

Moreover, he never in the decade-long series of attempts to play the Open sought to attain these necessary capabilities and credentials. Having dismissed and, it could be argued, distained the R&A's rules (and having taken advantage of the R&A's less than rigorous governance), he never earned the accolades he so enthusiastically pursued. Consequently, after 1976, despite all his subterfuge, he never again played a full round of golf in an Open qualifier.

The simple moral of Flitcroft's story is that to succeed, to deliver on a complex goal, requires more than just strategy. Strategy alone does not transform a crane operator into a professional golfer; nor does strategy alone transform a company from a basic level of performance to an optimized performance. Nor, it should be recognized, is desire or hope—as Flitcroft's story attests—a practical, achievable strategy.

In what may be a very insightful commentary on Flitcroft's endeavors, when told of his scoring a 121 at the Open, Flitcroft's mother, believing the high score implied victory, asked if he had won. When informed that not only had he not won, but the score was the worst in Open history, she replied "well, he has to start somewhere."[8] Unfortunately, presuming that one is starting at the top, as Flitcroft attempted, implies there is nowhere but down, and, conversely, that there is no opportunity or need to improve.

Believing that your company is at the pinnacle of performance is a harbinger of problems. It is this acceptance that no further improvement is needed or possible that results in complacency; while unnoticed due to that complacency, competitors can overtake you, customers can drift away, and market share can drop. It is often a function of complacency that, as Will Rogers so aptly put it, you get "run over."

As one 2018 study of American industry pointed out, changes in markets, ongoing disruptions, and evolving technology are continuously redefining corporate standings. Although in 1964, on average, a company could expect to remain on the S&P 500 index for 33 years, by 2016 that tenure had fallen to 24 years and was halved the following year to just 12. Based on their projections, this survey's authors concluded "about half of S&P 500 will be replaced" by 2028.[9]

So, where to start as you stand on the verge of this most important challenge for your company? Somewhat analogous to Archimedes' willingness to stand anywhere, a company does not necessarily need to begin its pursuit of optimization with the improvement of processes as we propose. Rather, the interlinking of—the interfaces among—operations and functions within a company allows for many potential points of entry. It's just our preference based on experience that process improvement serves as an effective starting point. It engages people representing a range of organizational assignments, thereby providing a natural springboard for spreading the management's message about its intention and its strategy. Yet, at the same time, because strategy is the central, unifying force for the optimization initiative, it allows for alternate points of initiating the enhancement effort.

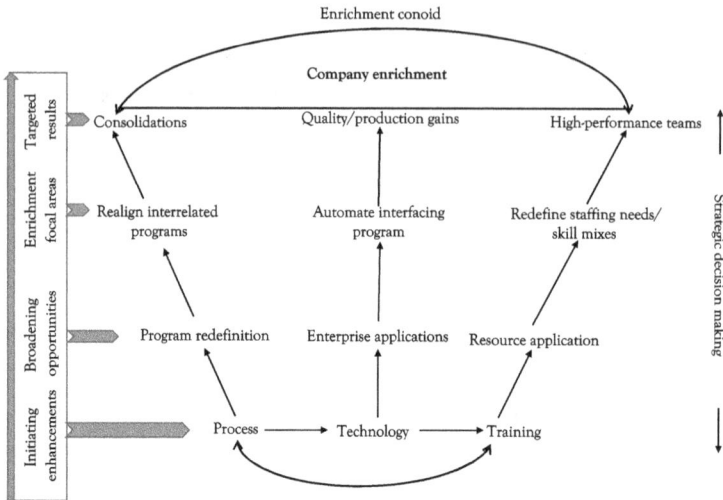

Figure 7.1 An integrated approach to company enrichment

To this end, Figure 7.1 (which we refer to as the "enrichment conoid") depicts the interactive logic of our approach to corporate optimization and company enrichment. Initial enhancements introduce broadening opportunities, which can then branch off into the intersecting communities, all connected through governance and the process of reasoned and disciplined strategic planning and decision making.

Ultimately, the path is guided by the strategies and decision making throughout the enrichment process that assess and monitor progress; evaluate opportunities for process improvement and technology gains; maintain alignment among organizational design and governance; and ensure a tight focus on the goals is maintained. Together, these factors coalesce into a self-perpetuating vehicle for the delivery of management's envisioned end point.

Given the perspectives, methodologies, and tools detailed in this text, you now have the opportunity to engage in a comprehensive rethinking and enrichment of your company or to engage in select, targeted enhancement initiatives. The initiation of the endeavor—the point from which you "tee off" your company's journey—now becomes a matter of your willingness to take ownership of the three guiding principles we asserted in the Introduction—principles that essentially form the equivalency of the overarching statement of your strategy:

The Vision: engaging all facets of the company in a shared effort to enhance the company's performance and sustainability

The Perspective: a comprehensive examination of all potential improvement opportunities both within the programs and in the interfaces among programs

The Practice: a full and complete endorsement of the use of the tools described in this text complemented by the power of the workforce—their expertise, experience, initiative, and energy

The path to corporate enhancement as these three components suggest is simple, but it is not easy; it takes determination and diligence. But with the tools and techniques, the power of the workforce, and the commitment of the management, it is achievable. It is, as we have experienced, a practical means to advance your company through all five facets of corporate optimization (process enhancement, personnel development, reasoned technological decisions, sound organizational alignment, and acting and thinking strategically) and through all phases from "Process Improvement to Company Enrichment."

Notes

Introduction

1. Plutarch (1899).
2. Meijer and Sleeswyk (1996), pp. 575–578.
3. Tzetzes (n.d.).
4. Russo (2013), pp. 91–95.
5. Shrader (2006).
6. McCloskey (n.d.), pp. 143–152.
7. Ibid.
8. Blackett (1962).
9. Subramanian, Scheff, Quillinan, Wiper, and Marsten (1994), pp. 104–120.
10. Rajgopal (2000).
11. Plung and Krull (2020).
12. Plung (2018).
13. Rajgopal (2000).
14. Babbage (1832).
15. Mason (2004), pp. 585–588.
16. INFORMS (n.d.).
17. Archimedes (n.d.).
18. U.S. Small Business Administration Office of Advocacy (2021).

Chapter 1

1. H.R. 5382 (n.d.).
2. Lighthall (1991), pp. 63–74.
3. Allianz Global Corporate & Specialty (2021).
4. Levine, Prosser, Evans, and Reicher (2005), pp. 443–453.
5. Batson and Ahmad (2002), pp. 429–445.
6. Bagehot (1877).
7. Parker (1993), pp. 105–112.

8. Colquitt (2007), pp. 1–51.
9. Baker (2022).
10. Morehead and Neck (1991), pp. 539–550.
11. Rogers (n.d.).
12. Toulmin (2003).

Chapter 2

1. Reid (1973).
2. Ibid.
3. Ibid.
4. Reid (2014).
5. Hoskins (2016).
6. Plung (2009).
7. Hoskins (2016).

Chapter 3

1. "The Pacific Railroad Complete Today" (1869).
2. Stanford University (n.d.).
3. Calver (1882).
4. Calver (1898).
5. "Are Steam and Electricity Doomed to Fall Before Concentrated Sunpower?" (1900).
6. "Has He Harnessed the Sun's Rays" (1900).
7. "Are Steam and Electricity Doomed to Fall Before Concentrated Sunpower?" (1900).
8. McGovern (1900), pp. 713–715.
9. Colorado Department of Transportation (CDOT) (2014).
10. Ibid.
11. CDOT (2014a).
12. Ibid.
13. CDOT (2014b).
14. DOT (2014).
15. Japan Rail Pass (2022).
16. Anderson (1975).

Chapter 4

1. Bailey (1921).
2. Makary and Daniel (2016).
3. Anupam and Prasad (2013).
4. Wallack and Chao (2001).
5. Bolster (2015), pp. 349–363.
6. Philibert and Amis (2011).
7. Kime and Anderson (1997).
8. Ibid.
9. Ibid.
10. Quoted in Fogg (2009).
11. Shulman (1987), pp. 1–22.
12. Ibid.
13. Kirkpatrick (1970).
14. Ibid.
15. Liao and Hsu (2019), pp. 266–279.
16. Smidt, Balandin, Sigafoos, and Reed (2009), pp. 266–274.
17. Surbhi (2014), pp. 19–30.
18. Moreau (2017), pp. 999–1001.

Chapter 5

1. "Captain Samuel Brown" (n.d.).
2. Jameson (1826).
3. Taylor and Phillips (1831), pp. 384–388.
4. Ibid.
5. Bender (1868).
6. Bender (1872).
7. Zyga (2010).
8. Mintzberg (1979).
9. Plung and Krull (2020).
10. Mintzberg (1979).
11. Ibid.
12. Ibid.
13. Ibid.

14. Ibid.
15. Gregory (2019).
16. Rainey (2022).
17. Meisenzahl (2021).
18. Rainey (2022).
19. Ibid.
20. Gregory (2019).

Chapter 6

1. Cornell (2010).
2. Ibid.
3. Ibid.
4. Rosenthal (2008).
5. Moore (2020).
6. Casey (2016).
7. *Detroit Times* (1914).
8. Ibid.
9. Ibid.
10. Gross (2014).
11. Adapted from Wooten and Horne (2001).

Chapter 7

1. Purdie and Dodd (2010).
2. Ibid.
3. Murray and Farnaby (2022).
4. de Quetteville (2014).
5. Ibid.
6. Ibid.
7. Murray and Farnaby (2022).
8. Ibid.
9. Anthony, Viguerie, Schwartz, and Van Landeghem (2018).

References

Allianz Global Corporate & Specialty. January 2021. "Allianz Risk Barometer for 2021." Allianz Global Corporate & Specialty, SE. www.agcs.allianz.com/news-and-insights/reports/allianz-risk-barometer.html.

Anderson, D.E. December 9, 1975. "Solar Energy Conversion System." US Patent 3,924,604.

Anthony, S.D., S.P. Viguerie, E.I. Schwartz, and J. Van Landeghem. February 2018. "2018 Corporate Longevity Forecast: Creative Destruction Is Accelerating." *Innosight*. https://www.innosight.com/insight/corporate-longevity-creative-destruction-is-accelerating

Anupam, B.J. and V. Prasad. April 2013. "Duty Hour Reform in a Shifting Medical Landscape." *Journal of General Internal Medicine*, pp. 1238–1240. https://doi.org/10.1007/s11606-013-2439-8.

Archimedes. n.d. *On Floating Bodies*, Book 1. Ed Thomas A Heath Cambridge University Press, 2010.

"Are Steam and Electricity Doomed to Fall Before Concentrated Sunpower?" February 4, 1990. *San Francisco Call*, Image 11. https://chroniclingamerica.loc.gov/lccn/sn85066387/1900-02-04/ed-1/seq-11/. From the Library of Congress, *Chronicling America*: Historic American Newspapers site.

Babbage, C. 1832. *On the Economy of Machinery and Manufactures*. Philadelphia: Carey & Lea. www.guternberg.org/cache/epub/4238/pg4238.html.

Bagehot, W. 1877. *The English Constitution and Other Political Essays*. New York, NY: D. Appleton and Company. https://archive.org/details/englishconstitu04bagegoog/page/n4/mode/2up.

Bailey, H. 1921. *Nursing Mental Diseases*. New York, NY: MacMillan. https://archive.org/details/3900206316237.med.yale.edu.

Baker, C. January 14, 2022. "14 Amazon Leadership Principles and Why They Matter." *Leaders*. https://leaders.com/articles/leadership/amazon-leadership-principles/.

Batson, C.D. and N. Ahmad. 2002. "Four Motives for Community Involvement." *Journal of Social Issues* 58, no. 3, pp. 429–445. www.baylor.edu/content/services/document.php/25043.pdf.

Bender, C. August 11, 1868. "Improvement in Suspension Bridges." Patent #71, 955. https://patentimages.storage.googleapis.com/d5/2d/32/50205f1f88bbd1/USRE3073.pdf.

Bender, C. 1872. "Historical Sketch of the Successive Improvements in Suspension Bridges to the Present." *Transactions of the American Society of Civil Engineers*, Vol. 1. New York, NY: American Society of Civil Engineers.

Blackett, P.M.S. 1962. "Scientists at the Operational Level." *Studies of War*, pp. 171–176. Edinburgh: Oliver and Boyd.

Bolster, R.L. September 2015. "The Effect of Restricting Residents' Duty Hours on Patient Safety, Resident Well-Being, and Resident Education: An Updated Systematic Review." *Journal of Graduate Medical Education* 7, no. 3, pp. 349–363. https://pubmed.ncbi.nlm.nih.gov/26457139/#:~:text=Most%20frequently%2C%20the%20studies%20concluded,on%20resident%20education%20(64%25).

Calver, W. July 4, 1882. "Method of and Means for Utilizing the Rays of the Sun." Patent US260,657.

Calver, W. May 3, 1898. "Solar Apparatus." Patent US603,317.

"Captain Samuel Brown." n.d. *Undiscovered Scotland.* https://undiscovered scotland.co.uk/usbiography/b/samuelbrown.html.

Casey, R. 2016. *The Model T: A Centennial History.* Baltimore, MD: Johns Hopkins University Press.

Colorado Department of Transportation (CDOT). April 2014. "Letters of Support From Clear Creek County and I70 Coalition." Appendix B, In *Advanced Guideway System (AGS) Feasibility Study.* https://codot.gov/projects/studies/study-archives/AGSstudy/final-ags-feasibility-study.

CDOT. 2014a. "Chapter 2 Technology Evaluation." In *AGS Feasibility Study.*

CDOT. 2014b. "Chapter 9 Conclusions and Recommendations." In *AGS Feasibility Study.*

Colquitt, J.A. November 2007. "Using Jury Questionnaires; (Ab)using Jurors." *Connecticut Law Review* 40, no. 1, pp. 1–51. https://papers.ssrn.com/sol3/papers.cfm?abstract_id=1018743.

Cornell. January 10, 2010. "How Milwaukee's Famous Beer Became Infamous." *Beer Connoisseur.* https://beerconnoisseur.com/articles/how-milwaukees-famous-beer-became-infamous.

de Quetteville, H. ed. 2014. "Maurice Flitcroft." In *Thinker, Failure, Soldier, Jailer.* London, UK: Aurum Press, Ltd.

Detroit Times. January 14, 1914. "Ford Workers Get $10,000,000." Vol. 1, p. 7. https://chroniclingamerica.loc.gov/lccn/sn83016689/1914-01-05/ed-1/seq-1/.

DOT. 2014. *2014 Annual Report.* https://codot.gov/programs/research/assets/AnnualReports/2014-division-of-transit-rail-annual-report.

Fogg, B.J. 2009. "A Behavior Model for Persuasive Design." https://tubular insights.com/wp-content/uploads/2009/06/page4_1.pdf?msclkid=2d09c 8c9a7ad11ecba713ac1aec87760.

Gregory, L. February 16, 2019. "Starbucks Coffee's Mission Statement and Vision Statement (An Analysis)." Panmore Institute. https://stories.starbucks .com/press/2015/starbucks-mission-and-values/.

Gross, D. January 6, 2014. "Henry Ford Understood That Raising Wages Would Bring Him More Profit." *Daily Beast*. www.thedailybeast.com/ henry-ford-understood-that-raising-wages-would-bring-him-more-profit#: ~:text=While%20paying%20higher%20wages%20than,business%20 and%20economy%20over%20time.

"Has He Harnessed the Sun's Rays." January 21, 1900. *St. Louis Republic* 11. https://chroniclingamerica.loc.gov/lccn/sn84020274/1900-01-21/ed-1/seq-47/. From the Library of Congress, *Chronicling America*: Historic American Newspapers site.

Hoskins, T. 2016. *Flight From Colditz*. Yorkshire, England: Frontline Books.

H.R. 5382. n.d. "Commercial Space Launch Amendments Act of 2004." www .congress.gov.bill/108th-congress/house-bill/5382/text.

INFORMS. n.d. *Management Science*. https://pubsonline.informs.orgpb/assets/ raw/mnsc-journal-flyer-152934069043.pdf.

Jameson, R. 1826. "Edinburgh Philosophical Journal, Vol XIV." https://www .biodiversitylibrary.org/page/50892559.

Japan Rail Pass. January 21, 2022. "The Japanese Maglev: World's Fastest Bullet Train." www.jrailpass.com/blog/maglev-bullet-train.

Kime, S.F. and C.L. Anderson. 1997. *Education vs. Training: A Military Perspective*. Servicemembers Opportunity Colleges. https://eric.ed.gov/?q= steve+f+kime&ID=ed404452.

Kirkpatrick, D. 1970. "Evaluation of Training." In *Evaluation of Short-Term Training in Rehabilitation*, ed. P.L. Browning. Eugene, Oregon: University of Oregon. https://eric.ed.gov/?q=Philip+L+Browning&id=ED057208.

Levine, M., A. Prosser, D. Evans, and S. Reicher. April 2005. "Identity and Emergency Intervention: How Social Group Membership and Inclusiveness of Group Boundaries Shape Helping Behavior." *Personality and Social Psychology* 31, no. 4, pp. 443–453. www.almendron.com/tribuna/wp-content/uploads/2016/12/Identity-and-Emergency-intervention.pdf.

Liao, S.C. and S.Y. Hsu. 2019. "Evaluating a Continuing Medical Education Program: New World Kirkpatrick Model." *International Journal of Management, Economics and Social Sciences* 8, no. 4, pp. 266–279.

Lighthall, F.F. February 1991. "Launching the Space Shuttle Challenger: Disciplinary Deficiencies in the Analysis of Engineering Data." *IEEE Transactions on Engineering Management* 38, no. 1, pp. 63–74.

Makary, M.A. and M. Daniel. May 3, 2016. "Study Suggests Medical Errors Now Third Leading Cause of Death in the U.S." *BMJ* 353. www.bmj.com/ content/353/bmj.i2139.

Mason, R.O. 2004. "IFORS' Operational Research Hall of Fame—C. West Churchman." *International Transactions in Operations Research* 11, pp. 585–588. https://onlinelibrary.wiley.com/doi/pdf/10.1111/j.1475-3995.2004.00478.x.

McCloskey, J.F. n.d. "The Beginnings of Operations Research 1934–1941." *Operations Research* 35, no. 1, pp. 143–152. https://doi.org/10.1287/opre .35.1.143.

McGovern, C.M. December 1900. "Tapping the Sun's Rays." *Pearsons Magazine* 4, no. 6, pp. 713–715. https://babel.hathitrust.org/cgi/ pt?id=njp.32101064077744&view=1up&seq=12&skin=2021.

Meijer, F. and A. Sleeswyk. December 1996. "On the Construction of the 'Syracusia.'" *Classical Quarterly* 46, no. 2, pp. 575–578.

Meisenzahl, M. September 4, 2021. "Starbucks Calls Its Workers 'Partners,' But Some Who Are Trying to Unionize Say the Chain Isn't Living Up to That Promise." *Business Insider.* https://ww.business-insider.com/starbucks-workers-say-they-aren't-true-oartners-2021-9#:~:text-starbuck%20employees %20are%20called%20partners%20because%20technically%2C%20they,units %20%28RSUs%29%2C%20which%do%20not%20carry%voting%rights.

Mintzberg, H. 1979. *The Structuring of Organization.* Hoboken, NJ: Prentice Hall.

Moore, S. May 25, 2020. "How the #2 Beer Company in America Self Destructed." *Medium.* https://bettermarketing.pub/how-the-2-beer-company-in-america-self-destructed-2bb8fa40a916.

Moreau, K.A. June 2017. "Has the New Kirkpatrick Generation Built a Better Hammer for Our Evaluation Toolbox?" *Medical Teacher* 39, no. 9, pp. 999–1001. https://pubmed.ncbi.nlm.nih.gov/28649887/.

Morehead, G. and C.P. Neck. June 1991. "Group Decision Fiascoes Continue: Space Shuttle Challenger and Revised Groupthink Framework." *Human Relations* 44, no. 6, pp. 539–550.

Murray, S. and S. Farnaby. 2022. *The Phantom of the Open: Maurice Flitcroft, the World's Worst Golfer.* Vintage.

Parker, W. 1993. "The Reasonable Person: A Gendered Concept?" *Victoria University of Wellington Law Review* 23, pp. 105–112. www6.austlii.edu.au/ nz/journals/VUWLawRw/1993/28.pdf.

Philibert, I. and S. Amis, ed. 2011. *The ACGME 2011 Duty Hour Standard Enhancing Quality of Care, Supervision and Resident Professional Development.* Accreditation Council for Graduate Medical Education (ACGME). http:// www.acgme-2010standard...monographs/jgme-monograph.pdf (citizen.org).

Plung, D. April 2018. "The Japanese Village at Dugway Proving Ground: An Unexamined Context to the Firebombing of Japan." *Asia Pacific Journal,* Japan Focus 16, issue 8, no. 3. https://apjjf.org/2018/08/plung.html.

Plung, D. November 2009. *Manual for the Reinvention of the Sellafield Management System,* SLM-4.5.1. Sellafield, England: Nuclear Management Partners.

Plung, D. and C. Krull. 2020. *The Practical Guide for Transforming Your Company.* New York, NY: Business Expert Press.

Plutarch. 1899. "Life of Marcellus." *Plutarch's Lives*, Vol. II, trans. A. Stewart. https:// www.gutenberg.org/ebooks/search/?query=life+of+marcellus&submit_ search=go!.

Purdie, D. and H. Dodd. 2010. *The Greatest Game: The Ancyent and Healthfulle Exercyse of the Golff.* Edinburgh, Scotland: Birlinn Ltd.

Rainey, C. March 22, 2022. "What Happened to Starbucks? How a Progressive Company Lost Its Way." *FastCompany.* www.fastcompany.com/90732166/ what-happened-to-starbucks-how-a-progressive-company-lost-its-way.

Rajgopal, J. 2000. "Principles and Applications of Operations Research." In *Maynard's Industrial Engineering Handbook*, ed. P. Harold, 5th edition. New York, NY: McGraw-Hill. https://sites.pitt.edu/~jrclass/or/or-intro .html#history.

Reid, P.R. 1973. *Escape From Colditz.* Philadelphia, PA: Lippincott.

Reid, P.R. 2014. *The Latter Days at Colditz.* London, England: Hodder and Stroughton.

Rogers, C.A. n.d. "Communication: Its Blocking and Its Facilitation." www .academia.edu/26501635/Communication_its_Blocking_and_Its_ Facilitaton.

Rosenthal, P. April 5, 2008. "The Ad That Made Schlitz Infamous." *Chicago Tribune.* www.chicagotribune.com/news/ct-xpm-2008-04-06-0804040774 -story.html.

Russo, L. October 2013. "Archimedes Between Legend and Fact." *Lettera Mathematica International,* pp. 91–95. www.researchgate.net/ publication/257810401_Archimedes_between_legend_and_fact.

Shrader, C.R. 2006. *History of Operations Research in the United States Army,* Vol. I, 1942–1962. Washington, D.C.: US Government Printing Office. https://history.army.mil/html/books/hist_op_research/index.html.

Shulman, L. 1987. "Knowledge and Teaching: Foundations of the New Reform." *Harvard Educational Review* 57, no.1, pp. 1–22.

Smidt, A., S. Balandin, J. Sigafoos, and V.A. Reed. September 2009. "The Kirkpatrick Model: A Useful Tool for Evaluating Training Outcomes." *Journal of Intellectual & Developmental Disability* 34, no. 3, pp. 266–274.

Stanford University: The Founding Grant with Amendments, Legislation, and Court Decries. n.d. https://purl.stanford.edu/bz978md4965.

Subramanian, R., R.P. Scheff, J.D. Quillinan, D.S. Wiper, and R.E. Marsten. January 1994. "Coldstart: Fleet Assignment at Delta Airline." *Interfaces* 24, no. 1, pp. 104–120.

Surbhi, J. April 2014. "Methods of Training Programmes Evaluation: A Review." *The Journal of Commerce* 6, no. 2, pp. 19–30.

Taylor, R. and R. Phillips. 1831. "Fall of the Broughton Suspension Bridge, near Manchester." In *The Philosophical Magazine or Annals of Chemistry,*

Mathematics, Astronomy, Natural History and General Science 9, pp. 384–388. London: Richard Taylor. https://archive.org/details/s2id13416500/page/n5/mode/2up.

"The Pacific Railroad Complete Today." May 10, 1869. *Chicago Tribune*. https://chroniclingamerica.loc.gov/lccn/sn82014064/1869-05-10/ed-1/seq-2/. From the Library of Congress, *Chronicling America*: Historic American Newspapers site.

Toulmin, S. 2003. *The Uses of Argument*. Cambridge, UK: Cambridge University Press.

Tzetzes, J. n.d. "Concerning Archimedes and Some of His Machines." In *The Chiliades*, Book 2, Section 2.3, trans. G. Berkowitz. https://www.theoi.com/Text/TzetzesChiliades2.html.

U.S. Small Business Administration Office of Advocacy. November 3, 2021. "Frequently Asked Questions About Small Business, 2021." https://advocacy.sba.gov.

Wallack, M.C. and L. Chao. 2001. "Resident Work Hours: The Evolution of a Revolution." *Arch Surg* 136, no. 12, pp. 1426–1432.

Wooten, S. and T. Horne. 2001. *Strategic Thinking: A Step-By-Step Approach to Strategy*. London, UK: Kagan Page.

Zyga, L. February 8, 2010. "Physicists Investigate Structural Properties of Spider Webs." *Phy.org*. https://phys.org/news/2010-02-physicists-properties-spider-webs.html.

About the Authors

Dr. Daniel L. Plung has 40+ years of leadership experience in a variety of U.K. and U.S. corporations, with responsibility for all project phases from proposal development to contract closeout. Trained in both Lean and Six Sigma, Dr. Plung is a recognized expert in process optimization, a skill he has applied to the transformation of government contracts as well as to commercial and nonprofit companies. Dr. Plung has served on the faculty of three major universities, on corporate boards, and on the Washington State Board of Education. He has authored more than 50 publications, including two anthologies, a college textbook on professional communication, and—as coauthor with Connie Krull—the Business Expert Press publication, *The Practical Guide to Transforming Your Company*.

Connie Krull has more than 25+ years of experience supporting and managing infrastructure and operations activities. She has had a succession of assignments focused on strategic management and strategic planning, while effectively implementing long-term business strategies and optimizing internal operations. Trained in both Lean and Six Sigma, Ms. Krull specializes in taking a systematic approach to identifying and implementing organizational change and ensuring a successful implementation of change management and organizational transformation.

Index

OTHER TITLES IN THE SUPPLY AND OPERATIONS MANAGEMENT COLLECTION

Joy M. Field, Boston College, Editor

- *Organizational Velocity* by Alan Amling
- *C-O-S-T* by Craig Theisen
- *RFID for the Supply Chain and Operations Professional, Third Edition* by Pamela J. Zelbst and Victor Sower
- *Operations Management in China, Second Edition* by Craig Seidelson
- *Futureproofing Procurement* by Katie Jarvis-Grove
- *How Efficiency Changes the Game* by Ray Hodge
- *Supply Chain Planning, Second Edition* by Matthew J. Liberatore and Tan Miller
- *Sustainable Quality* by Joseph Diele
- *Why Quality is Important and How It Applies in Diverse Business and Social Environments, Volume II* by Paul Hayes
- *Why Quality is Important and How It Applies in Diverse Business and Social Environments, Volume I* by Paul Hayes
- *The Cost* by Chris Domanski

Concise and Applied Business Books

The Collection listed above is one of 30 business subject collections that Business Expert Press has grown to make BEP a premiere publisher of print and digital books. Our concise and applied books are for...

- Professionals and Practitioners
- Faculty who adopt our books for courses
- Librarians who know that BEP's Digital Libraries are a unique way to offer students ebooks to download, not restricted with any digital rights management
- Executive Training Course Leaders
- Business Seminar Organizers

Business Expert Press books are for anyone who needs to dig deeper on business ideas, goals, and solutions to everyday problems. Whether one print book, one ebook, or buying a digital library of 110 ebooks, we remain the affordable and smart way to be business smart. For more information, please visit www.businessexpertpress.com, or contact sales@businessexpertpress.com.

www.ingramcontent.com/pod-product-compliance
Lightning Source LLC
Chambersburg PA
CBHW061218220326
41599CB00025B/4676